Republican Budget Resolutions: Same Failed Top-Down Economics for Alabama

With more than 12 million private-sector jobs created over the last 60 months, it is clear that the President's middle class economic agenda is working. But instead of taking the steps we need to strengthen the standing of working families, the Republican budgets for fiscal year (FY) 2016 would return our economy to the same top-down economics that has failed us before: cutting taxes for millionaires and billionaires, while slashing investments in the middle class that we need to grow the economy, like education, job training, and manufacturing. The Republican proposals stand in stark contrast to the President's FY 2016 Budget, which would bring middle class economics into the 21st Century. A state-by-state breakdown of this contrast, including how the Republican budgets affect Alabama, can be found in a report released today here: http://go.wh.gov/RoNU1j.

The President's Budget builds on the progress we've made and shows what we can do if we invest in America's future and commit to an economy that rewards hard work, generates rising incomes, and allows everyone to share in the prosperity of a growing America. It lays out a strategy to strengthen our middle class and help America's hard-working families get ahead in a time of relentless economic and technological change. And it makes the critical investments needed to accelerate and sustain economic growth in the long run, including in research, education, training, and infrastructure.

Republicans have chosen different priorities. Yet again, they are seeking to balance the budget on the backs of the middle class, while cutting taxes for the wealthy and well-connected. They still won't say where many of their spending cuts come from. But they are clear that their budgets would continue the harmful cuts known as sequestration in 2016, threatening economic growth, cutting programs middle-class families count on, and attempting to fund national security through irresponsible budget gimmicks. Their budgets slash domestic investments that support the middle-class even more significantly after 2016, along with programs that serve the most vulnerable Americans. House Republicans would end Medicare as we know it, transforming it from a guarantee seniors can count on into a voucher program. After five years of the Affordable Care Act, more than 16 million people have gained coverage. Yet once again, the Republican budgets propose to repeal the Affordable Care Act's coverage expansions.

The choice could not be more clear or the consequences more stark. Thanks to President Obama and the resilience of the American people, the economy is growing

again. The Republican budgets would put that growth at risk and limit opportunity for the middle-class and those seeking to join it.

In Alabama, the Republican budgets would[i]:

Cut Taxes for Millionaires and Raise Taxes for Working Families and Students: While claiming to prioritize fiscal responsibility, the Republican budgets would not ask the wealthy to contribute a single dollar to deficit reduction, and the proposals specified in the House budget would cut taxes for millionaires by an average of at least $50,000. Meanwhile, the Republican budgets do nothing to prevent tax increases averaging $1,100 for 12 million families and students paying for college and $900 for 16 million working families with children. In 2015, 304,000 Alabama families will receive a total of $274 million in tax cuts from improvements to pro-work tax credits that would expire after 2017 under the Republican budgets.

Eliminate Affordable Health Care: The Affordable Care Act is working. After five years of the Affordable Care Act, more than 16 million people have gained coverage. Yet once again, the Republican budgets propose to repeal the Affordable Care Act's coverage expansions, taking away health insurance from millions of people. In particular, the Republican budgets would eliminate coverage for 172,000 Alabama residents who have newly signed up for coverage or re-enrolled through the Marketplaces. Some of these individuals would become uninsured while others would end up with worse or less affordable coverage.

Raise Health Care Costs for Seniors: 89,300 Alabama seniors and people with disabilities benefited by an average of $930 from the closure of the Medicare Part D prescription drug donut hole in 2014 alone. Under the Republican plan to repeal the Affordable Care Act, at least that many would likely have to pay more for needed medications in future years. The House budget would also end Medicare as we know it, replacing guaranteed access to the traditional Medicare program with a voucher program, risking a death spiral in traditional Medicare.

Slash Investments in the Middle Class: Under the Republican budgets, both non-defense and base defense discretionary funding in 2016 would be at the lowest real levels in a decade. Compared to the President's Budget, if the Republican budgets were to take effect, these are just some of the impacts on Alabama:

- **Head Start:** 570 fewer children in Alabama would have access to Head Start services, representing a permanently missed opportunity to help these children enter elementary school ready to succeed.
- **Teachers and Schools:** Alabama would receive $17.9 million less funding for disadvantaged students, an amount that is enough to fund about 70 schools, 250 teacher and aide jobs, and 34,000 students.

- **Education for Children with Disabilities:** Alabama would receive $5.1 million less funding to provide educational opportunities for students with disabilities, representing an approximately 2.8 percent cut and shifting the burden for meeting these children's needs to Alabama and its local communities.
- **Job Training and Employment Services:** 28,900 fewer Alabama residents would receive job training and employment services, including help finding jobs and skills training.
- **Affordable Housing**: Alabama would receive approximately $17.6 million less in Federal funding, resulting in 1,840 fewer families receiving Housing Choice Vouchers, which enable very low-income families to afford decent, safe, and sanitary housing in the private market.
- **National Parks:** Construction and renovation projects would be prevented or delayed at two national parks in Alabama: Horseshoe Bend National Military Park and the Selma to Montgomery Historic Trail.

Balances Only with Gimmicks and Deep Cuts to Programs that Serve the Most Vulnerable and Help Expand Opportunity. On top of their cuts to middle-class investments and the ACA, the Republican budgets would cut:

- **Pell Grants:** Republican reductions to Pell would reduce financial aid for the 153,000 Alabama students who rely on Pell grants to afford college.
- **Medicaid:** The House Republican proposal to block grant Medicaid would cut Federal funding to Alabama by approximately $11.6 billion over ten years, impacting children, seniors, and people with disabilities who rely on Medicaid.
- **Supplemental Nutrition Assistance Program (SNAP):** House Republican proposals to block grant and slash SNAP would cut nutrition aid in Alabama by an estimated $2.1 billion over a five year period (2021-2025), jeopardizing nutrition assistance for the 902,000 Alabama residents who receive SNAP to help them put food on the table.

Fails to Address Our Crumbling Infrastructure: Republican budgets lack a real plan to address the looming expiration and insolvency of the Highway Trust Fund. Through the Highway Trust Fund, in FY 2014 the Federal Government obligated $824.5 million to Alabama through the Federal Aid Highways program for highway planning and construction and over $54.1 million through Transit Formula Grants that support our Nation's mass transit systems.

i. Numbers are rounded. For a description of how impacts were calculated, see http://go.wh.gov/RoNU1

THE WHITE HOUSE

Office of the Press Secretary

FOR IMMEDIATE RELEASE

March 24, 2015

FACT SHEET: Republican Budget Resolutions: Same Failed Top-Down Economics for Alaska

With more than 12 million private-sector jobs created over the last 60 months, it is clear that the President's middle class economic agenda is working. But instead of taking the steps we need to strengthen the standing of working families, the Republican budgets for fiscal year (FY) 2016 would return our economy to the same top-down economics that has failed us before: cutting taxes for millionaires and billionaires, while slashing investments in the middle class that we need to grow the economy, like education, job training, and manufacturing. The Republican proposals stand in stark contrast to the President's FY 2016 Budget, which would bring middle class economics into the 21st Century. A state-by-state breakdown of this contrast, including how the Republican budgets affect Alaska, can be found in a report released today here: http://go.wh.gov/RoNU1j.

The President's Budget builds on the progress we've made and shows what we can do if we invest in America's future and commit to an economy that rewards hard work, generates rising incomes, and allows everyone to share in the prosperity of a growing America. It lays out a strategy to strengthen our middle class and help America's hard-working families get ahead in a time of relentless economic and technological change. And it makes the critical investments needed to accelerate and sustain economic growth in the long run, including in research, education, training, and infrastructure.

Republicans have chosen different priorities. Yet again, they are seeking to balance the budget on the backs of the middle class, while cutting taxes for the wealthy and well-connected. They still won't say where many of their spending cuts come from. But they are clear that their budgets would continue the harmful cuts known as sequestration in 2016, threatening economic growth, cutting programs middle-class families count on, and attempting to fund national security through irresponsible budget gimmicks. Their budgets slash domestic investments that support the middle-class even more significantly after 2016, along with programs that serve the most vulnerable Americans. House Republicans would end Medicare as we know it, transforming it from a guarantee seniors can count on into a voucher program. After five years of the Affordable Care Act, more than 16 million people have gained coverage. Yet once again, the Republican budgets propose to repeal the Affordable Care Act's coverage expansions.

The choice could not be more clear or the consequences more stark. Thanks to President Obama and the resilience of the American people, the economy is growing

again. The Republican budgets would put that growth at risk and limit opportunity for the middle-class and those seeking to join it.

In Alaska, the Republican budgets would[i]:

Cut Taxes for Millionaires and Raise Taxes for Working Families and Students:
While claiming to prioritize fiscal responsibility, the Republican budgets would not ask the wealthy to contribute a single dollar to deficit reduction, and the proposals specified in the House budget would cut taxes for millionaires by an average of at least $50,000. Meanwhile, the Republican budgets do nothing to prevent tax increases averaging $1,100 for 12 million families and students paying for college and $900 for 16 million working families with children. In 2015, 27,000 Alaska families will receive a total of $24 million in tax cuts from improvements to pro-work tax credits that would expire after 2017 under the Republican budgets.

Eliminate Affordable Health Care: The Affordable Care Act is working. After five years of the Affordable Care Act, more than 16 million people have gained coverage. Yet once again, the Republican budgets propose to repeal the Affordable Care Act's coverage expansions, taking away health insurance from millions of people. In particular, the Republican budgets would eliminate coverage for 21,000 Alaska residents who have newly signed up for coverage or re-enrolled through the Marketplaces. Some of these individuals would become uninsured while others would end up with worse or less affordable coverage.

Raise Health Care Costs for Seniors: 3,200 Alaska seniors and people with disabilities benefited by an average of $960 from the closure of the Medicare Part D prescription drug donut hole in 2014 alone. Under the Republican plan to repeal the Affordable Care Act, at least that many would likely have to pay more for needed medications in future years. The House budget would also end Medicare as we know it, replacing guaranteed access to the traditional Medicare program with a voucher program, risking a death spiral in traditional Medicare.

Slash Investments in the Middle Class: Under the Republican budgets, both non-defense and base defense discretionary funding in 2016 would be at the lowest real levels in a decade. Compared to the President's Budget, if the Republican budgets were to take effect, these are just some of the impacts on Alaska:

- **Head Start:** 70 fewer children in Alaska would have access to Head Start services, representing a permanently missed opportunity to help these children enter elementary school ready to succeed.
- **Teachers and Schools:** Alaska would receive $3.5 million less funding for disadvantaged students, an amount that is enough to fund about 20 schools, 50 teacher and aide jobs, and 4,000 students.

- **Education for Children with Disabilities:** Alaska would receive $1.2 million less funding to provide educational opportunities for students with disabilities, representing an approximately 3.2 percent cut and shifting the burden for meeting these children's needs to Alaska and its local communities.
- **Job Training and Employment Services:** 24,500 fewer Alaska residents would receive job training and employment services, including help finding jobs and skills training.
- **Affordable Housing**: Alaska would receive approximately $3.5 million less in Federal funding, resulting in 240 fewer families receiving Housing Choice Vouchers, which enable very low-income families to afford decent, safe, and sanitary housing in the private market.
- **National Parks:** Construction and renovation projects would be prevented or delayed at seven national parks in Alaska: Denali National Park and Preserve, Glacier Bay National Park and Preserve, Katmai National Park and Preserve, Kenai Fjords National Park, Klondike Gold Rush National Historic Park, Sitka National Historic Park, and Wrangell-Saint Elias National Park and Preserve.

Balances Only with Gimmicks and Deep Cuts to Programs that Serve the Most Vulnerable and Help Expand Opportunity. On top of their cuts to middle-class investments and the ACA, the Republican budgets would cut:

- **Pell Grants:** Republican reductions to Pell would reduce financial aid for the 11,000 Alaska students who rely on Pell grants to afford college.
- **Medicaid:** The House Republican proposal to block grant Medicaid would cut Federal funding to Alaska by approximately $2.8 billion over ten years, impacting children, seniors, and people with disabilities who rely on Medicaid.
- **Supplemental Nutrition Assistance Program (SNAP):** House Republican proposals to block grant and slash SNAP would cut nutrition aid in Alaska by an estimated $300 million over a five year period (2021-2025), jeopardizing nutrition assistance for the 87,000 Alaska residents who receive SNAP to help them put food on the table.

Fails to Address Our Crumbling Infrastructure: Republican budgets lack a real plan to address the looming expiration and insolvency of the Highway Trust Fund. Through the Highway Trust Fund, in FY 2014 the Federal Government obligated $582.5 million to Alaska through the Federal Aid Highways program for highway planning and construction and over $68.9 million through Transit Formula Grants that support our Nation's mass transit systems.

###

i. Numbers are rounded. For a description of how impacts were calculated, see http://go.wh.gov/RoNU1j

FOR IMMEDIATE RELEASE
March 24, 2015

FACT SHEET: Republican Budget Resolutions: Same Failed Top-Down Economics for Arizona

With more than 12 million private-sector jobs created over the last 60 months, it is clear that the President's middle class economic agenda is working. But instead of taking the steps we need to strengthen the standing of working families, the Republican budgets for fiscal year (FY) 2016 would return our economy to the same top-down economics that has failed us before: cutting taxes for millionaires and billionaires, while slashing investments in the middle class that we need to grow the economy, like education, job training, and manufacturing. The Republican proposals stand in stark contrast to the President's FY 2016 Budget, which would bring middle class economics into the 21st Century. A state-by-state breakdown of this contrast, including how the Republican budgets affect Arizona, can be found in a report released today here: http://go.wh.gov/RoNU1j.

The President's Budget builds on the progress we've made and shows what we can do if we invest in America's future and commit to an economy that rewards hard work, generates rising incomes, and allows everyone to share in the prosperity of a growing America. It lays out a strategy to strengthen our middle class and help America's hard-working families get ahead in a time of relentless economic and technological change. And it makes the critical investments needed to accelerate and sustain economic growth in the long run, including in research, education, training, and infrastructure.

Republicans have chosen different priorities. Yet again, they are seeking to balance the budget on the backs of the middle class, while cutting taxes for the wealthy and well-connected. They still won't say where many of their spending cuts come from. But they are clear that their budgets would continue the harmful cuts known as sequestration in 2016, threatening economic growth, cutting programs middle-class families count on, and attempting to fund national security through irresponsible budget gimmicks. Their budgets slash domestic investments that support the middle-class even more significantly after 2016, along with programs that serve the most vulnerable Americans. House Republicans would end Medicare as we know it, transforming it from a guarantee seniors can count on into a voucher program. After five years of the Affordable Care Act, more than 16 million people have gained coverage. Yet once again, the Republican budgets propose to repeal the Affordable Care Act's coverage expansions.

The choice could not be more clear or the consequences more stark. Thanks to President Obama and the resilience of the American people, the economy is growing

again. The Republican budgets would put that growth at risk and limit opportunity for the middle-class and those seeking to join it.

In Arizona, the Republican budgets would[i]:

Cut Taxes for Millionaires and Raise Taxes for Working Families and Students: While claiming to prioritize fiscal responsibility, the Republican budgets would not ask the wealthy to contribute a single dollar to deficit reduction, and the proposals specified in the House budget would cut taxes for millionaires by an average of at least $50,000. Meanwhile, the Republican budgets do nothing to prevent tax increases averaging $1,100 for 12 million families and students paying for college and $900 for 16 million working families with children. In 2015, 359,000 Arizona families will receive a total of $345 million in tax cuts from improvements to pro-work tax credits that would expire after 2017 under the Republican budgets.

Eliminate Affordable Health Care: The Affordable Care Act is working. After five years of the Affordable Care Act, more than 16 million people have gained coverage. Yet once again, the Republican budgets propose to repeal the Affordable Care Act's coverage expansions, taking away health insurance from millions of people. In particular, the Republican budgets would eliminate coverage for 206,000 Arizona residents who have newly signed up for coverage or re-enrolled through the Marketplaces. Some of these individuals would become uninsured while others would end up with worse or less affordable coverage.

Raise Health Care Costs for Seniors: 95,200 Arizona seniors and people with disabilities benefited by an average of $870 from the closure of the Medicare Part D prescription drug donut hole in 2014 alone. Under the Republican plan to repeal the Affordable Care Act, at least that many would likely have to pay more for needed medications in future years. The House budget would also end Medicare as we know it, replacing guaranteed access to the traditional Medicare program with a voucher program, risking a death spiral in traditional Medicare.

Slash Investments in the Middle Class: Under the Republican budgets, both non-defense and base defense discretionary funding in 2016 would be at the lowest real levels in a decade. Compared to the President's Budget, if the Republican budgets were to take effect, these are just some of the impacts on Arizona:

- **Head Start:** 560 fewer children in Arizona would have access to Head Start services, representing a permanently missed opportunity to help these children enter elementary school ready to succeed.
- **Teachers and Schools:** Arizona would receive $27.3 million less funding for disadvantaged students, an amount that is enough to fund about 100 schools, 370 teacher and aide jobs, and 22,000 students.

- **Education for Children with Disabilities:** Arizona would receive $8.8 million less funding to provide educational opportunities for students with disabilities, representing an approximately 4.5 percent cut and shifting the burden for meeting these children's needs to Arizona and its local communities.
- **Job Training and Employment Services:** 42,500 fewer Arizona residents would receive job training and employment services, including help finding jobs and skills training.
- **Affordable Housing**: Arizona would receive approximately $15.9 million less in Federal funding, resulting in 1,370 fewer families receiving Housing Choice Vouchers, which enable very low-income families to afford decent, safe, and sanitary housing in the private market.
- **National Parks:** Construction and renovation projects would be prevented or delayed at eight national parks in Arizona: Casa Grande Ruins National Monument, Fort Bowie National Historic Site, Glen Canyon National Recreation Area, Grand Canyon National Park, Grand Canyon-Parashant National Monument, Petrified Forest National Park, Wupatki National Monument, and Saguro National Park.

Balances Only with Gimmicks and Deep Cuts to Programs that Serve the Most Vulnerable and Help Expand Opportunity. On top of their cuts to middle-class investments and the ACA, the Republican budgets would cut:

- **Pell Grants:** Republican reductions to Pell would reduce financial aid for the 403,000 Arizona students who rely on Pell grants to afford college.
- **Medicaid:** The House Republican proposal to block grant Medicaid would cut Federal funding to Arizona by approximately $20.9 billion over ten years, impacting children, seniors, and people with disabilities who rely on Medicaid.
- **Supplemental Nutrition Assistance Program (SNAP):** House Republican proposals to block grant and slash SNAP would cut nutrition aid in Arizona by an estimated $2.3 billion over a five year period (2021-2025), jeopardizing nutrition assistance for the 1,044,000 Arizona residents who receive SNAP to help them put food on the table.

Fails to Address Our Crumbling Infrastructure: Republican budgets lack a real plan to address the looming expiration and insolvency of the Highway Trust Fund. Through the Highway Trust Fund, in FY 2014 the Federal Government obligated $747.3 million to Arizona through the Federal Aid Highways program for highway planning and construction and over $148.2 million through Transit Formula Grants that support our Nation's mass transit systems.

i. Numbers are rounded. For a description of how impacts were calculated, see http://go.wh.gov/RoNU1j

FOR IMMEDIATE RELEASE
March 24, 2015

FACT SHEET: Republican Budget Resolutions: Same Failed Top-Down Economics for Arkansas

With more than 12 million private-sector jobs created over the last 60 months, it is clear that the President's middle class economic agenda is working. But instead of taking the steps we need to strengthen the standing of working families, the Republican budgets for fiscal year (FY) 2016 would return our economy to the same top-down economics that has failed us before: cutting taxes for millionaires and billionaires, while slashing investments in the middle class that we need to grow the economy, like education, job training, and manufacturing. The Republican proposals stand in stark contrast to the President's FY 2016 Budget, which would bring middle class economics into the 21st Century. A state-by-state breakdown of this contrast, including how the Republican budgets affect Arkansas, can be found in a report released today here: http://go.wh.gov/RoNU1j.

The President's Budget builds on the progress we've made and shows what we can do if we invest in America's future and commit to an economy that rewards hard work, generates rising incomes, and allows everyone to share in the prosperity of a growing America. It lays out a strategy to strengthen our middle class and help America's hard-working families get ahead in a time of relentless economic and technological change. And it makes the critical investments needed to accelerate and sustain economic growth in the long run, including in research, education, training, and infrastructure.

Republicans have chosen different priorities. Yet again, they are seeking to balance the budget on the backs of the middle class, while cutting taxes for the wealthy and well-connected. They still won't say where many of their spending cuts come from. But they are clear that their budgets would continue the harmful cuts known as sequestration in 2016, threatening economic growth, cutting programs middle-class families count on, and attempting to fund national security through irresponsible budget gimmicks. Their budgets slash domestic investments that support the middle-class even more significantly after 2016, along with programs that serve the most vulnerable Americans. House Republicans would end Medicare as we know it, transforming it from a guarantee seniors can count on into a voucher program. After five years of the Affordable Care Act, more than 16 million people have gained coverage. Yet once again, the Republican budgets propose to repeal the Affordable Care Act's coverage expansions.

The choice could not be more clear or the consequences more stark. Thanks to President Obama and the resilience of the American people, the economy is growing

again. The Republican budgets would put that growth at risk and limit opportunity for the middle-class and those seeking to join it.

In Arkansas, the Republican budgets would[i]:

Cut Taxes for Millionaires and Raise Taxes for Working Families and Students: While claiming to prioritize fiscal responsibility, the Republican budgets would not ask the wealthy to contribute a single dollar to deficit reduction, and the proposals specified in the House budget would cut taxes for millionaires by an average of at least $50,000. Meanwhile, the Republican budgets do nothing to prevent tax increases averaging $1,100 for 12 million families and students paying for college and $900 for 16 million working families with children. In 2015, 179,000 Arkansas families will receive a total of $161 million in tax cuts from improvements to pro-work tax credits that would expire after 2017 under the Republican budgets.

Eliminate Affordable Health Care: The Affordable Care Act is working. After five years of the Affordable Care Act, more than 16 million people have gained coverage. Yet once again, the Republican budgets propose to repeal the Affordable Care Act's coverage expansions, taking away health insurance from millions of people. In particular, the Republican budgets would eliminate coverage for 66,000 Arkansas residents who have newly signed up for coverage or re-enrolled through the Marketplaces. Some of these individuals would become uninsured while others would end up with worse or less affordable coverage.

Raise Health Care Costs for Seniors: 40,500 Arkansas seniors and people with disabilities benefited by an average of $780 from the closure of the Medicare Part D prescription drug donut hole in 2014 alone. Under the Republican plan to repeal the Affordable Care Act, at least that many would likely have to pay more for needed medications in future years. The House budget would also end Medicare as we know it, replacing guaranteed access to the traditional Medicare program with a voucher program, risking a death spiral in traditional Medicare.

Slash Investments in the Middle Class: Under the Republican budgets, both non-defense and base defense discretionary funding in 2016 would be at the lowest real levels in a decade. Compared to the President's Budget, if the Republican budgets were to take effect, these are just some of the impacts on Arkansas:

- **Head Start:** 330 fewer children in Arkansas would have access to Head Start services, representing a permanently missed opportunity to help these children enter elementary school ready to succeed.
- **Teachers and Schools:** Arkansas would receive $11.7 million less funding for disadvantaged students, an amount that is enough to fund about 60 schools, 160 teacher and aide jobs, and 20,000 students.

- **Education for Children with Disabilities:** Arkansas would receive $3.2 million less funding to provide educational opportunities for students with disabilities, representing an approximately 2.9 percent cut and shifting the burden for meeting these children's needs to Arkansas and its local communities.
- **Job Training and Employment Services:** 18,000 fewer Arkansas residents would receive job training and employment services, including help finding jobs and skills training.
- **Affordable Housing:** Arkansas would receive approximately $8.8 million less in Federal funding, resulting in 1,220 fewer families receiving Housing Choice Vouchers, which enable very low-income families to afford decent, safe, and sanitary housing in the private market.
- **National Parks:** Construction and renovation projects would be prevented or delayed at two national parks in Arkansas: Buffalo National River and Hot Springs National Park.

Balances Only with Gimmicks and Deep Cuts to Programs that Serve the Most Vulnerable and Help Expand Opportunity. On top of their cuts to middle-class investments and the ACA, the Republican budgets would cut:

- **Pell Grants:** Republican reductions to Pell would reduce financial aid for the 83,000 Arkansas students who rely on Pell grants to afford college.
- **Medicaid:** The House Republican proposal to block grant Medicaid would cut Federal funding to Arkansas by approximately $11.8 billion over ten years, impacting children, seniors, and people with disabilities who rely on Medicaid.
- **Supplemental Nutrition Assistance Program (SNAP):** House Republican proposals to block grant and slash SNAP would cut nutrition aid in Arkansas by an estimated $1.1 billion over a five year period (2021-2025), jeopardizing nutrition assistance for the 492,000 Arkansas residents who receive SNAP to help them put food on the table.

Fails to Address Our Crumbling Infrastructure: Republican budgets lack a real plan to address the looming expiration and insolvency of the Highway Trust Fund. Through the Highway Trust Fund, in FY 2014 the Federal Government obligated $550.3 million to Arkansas through the Federal Aid Highways program for highway planning and construction and over $32.3 million through Transit Formula Grants that support our Nation's mass transit systems.

i.   Numbers are rounded. For a description of how impacts were calculated, see http://go.wh.gov/RoNU1j

FOR IMMEDIATE RELEASE
March 24, 2015

FACT SHEET: Republican Budget Resolutions: Same Failed Top-Down Economics for California

With more than 12 million private-sector jobs created over the last 60 months, it is clear that the President's middle class economic agenda is working. But instead of taking the steps we need to strengthen the standing of working families, the Republican budgets for fiscal year (FY) 2016 would return our economy to the same top-down economics that has failed us before: cutting taxes for millionaires and billionaires, while slashing investments in the middle class that we need to grow the economy, like education, job training, and manufacturing. The Republican proposals stand in stark contrast to the President's FY 2016 Budget, which would bring middle class economics into the 21st Century. A state-by-state breakdown of this contrast, including how the Republican budgets affect California, can be found in a report released today here: http://go.wh.gov/RoNU1j.

The President's Budget builds on the progress we've made and shows what we can do if we invest in America's future and commit to an economy that rewards hard work, generates rising incomes, and allows everyone to share in the prosperity of a growing America. It lays out a strategy to strengthen our middle class and help America's hard-working families get ahead in a time of relentless economic and technological change. And it makes the critical investments needed to accelerate and sustain economic growth in the long run, including in research, education, training, and infrastructure.

Republicans have chosen different priorities. Yet again, they are seeking to balance the budget on the backs of the middle class, while cutting taxes for the wealthy and well-connected. They still won't say where many of their spending cuts come from. But they are clear that their budgets would continue the harmful cuts known as sequestration in 2016, threatening economic growth, cutting programs middle-class families count on, and attempting to fund national security through irresponsible budget gimmicks. Their budgets slash domestic investments that support the middle-class even more significantly after 2016, along with programs that serve the most vulnerable Americans. House Republicans would end Medicare as we know it, transforming it from a guarantee seniors can count on into a voucher program. After five years of the Affordable Care Act, more than 16 million people have gained coverage. Yet once again, the Republican budgets propose to repeal the Affordable Care Act's coverage expansions.

The choice could not be more clear or the consequences more stark. Thanks to President Obama and the resilience of the American people, the economy is growing

again. The Republican budgets would put that growth at risk and limit opportunity for the middle-class and those seeking to join it.

In California, the Republican budgets would[i]:

Cut Taxes for Millionaires and Raise Taxes for Working Families and Students: While claiming to prioritize fiscal responsibility, the Republican budgets would not ask the wealthy to contribute a single dollar to deficit reduction, and the proposals specified in the House budget would cut taxes for millionaires by an average of at least $50,000. Meanwhile, the Republican budgets do nothing to prevent tax increases averaging $1,100 for 12 million families and students paying for college and $900 for 16 million working families with children. In 2015, nearly 2 million California families will receive a total of $1.8 billion in tax cuts from improvements to pro-work tax credits that would expire after 2017 under the Republican budgets.

Eliminate Affordable Health Care: The Affordable Care Act is working. After five years of the Affordable Care Act, more than 16 million people have gained coverage. Yet once again, the Republican budgets propose to repeal the Affordable Care Act's coverage expansions, taking away health insurance from millions of people. In particular, the Republican budgets would eliminate coverage for more than 1.4 million California residents who have newly signed up for coverage or re-enrolled through the Marketplaces. Some of these individuals would become uninsured while others would end up with worse or less affordable coverage.

Raise Health Care Costs for Seniors: 417,500 California seniors and people with disabilities benefited by an average of $940 from the closure of the Medicare Part D prescription drug donut hole in 2014 alone. Under the Republican plan to repeal the Affordable Care Act, at least that many would likely have to pay more for needed medications in future years. The House budget would also end Medicare as we know it, replacing guaranteed access to the traditional Medicare program with a voucher program, risking a death spiral in traditional Medicare.

Slash Investments in the Middle Class: Under the Republican budgets, both non-defense and base defense discretionary funding in 2016 would be at the lowest real levels in a decade. Compared to the President's Budget, if the Republican budgets were to take effect, these are just some of the impacts on California:

- **Head Start:** 4,510 fewer children in California would have access to Head Start services, representing a permanently missed opportunity to help these children enter elementary school ready to succeed.
- **Teachers and Schools:** California would receive $147.6 million less funding for disadvantaged students, an amount that is enough to fund about 500 schools, 2,030 teacher and aide jobs, and 293,000 students.

- **Education for Children with Disabilities:** California would receive $35.3 million less funding to provide educational opportunities for students with disabilities, representing an approximately 2.9 percent cut and shifting the burden for meeting these children's needs to California and its local communities.
- **Job Training and Employment Services:** 269,800 fewer California residents would receive job training and employment services, including help finding jobs and skills training.
- **Affordable Housing**: California would receive approximately $321.2 million less in Federal funding, resulting in 18,530 fewer families receiving Housing Choice Vouchers, which enable very low-income families to afford decent, safe, and sanitary housing in the private market.
- **National Parks:** Construction and renovation projects would be prevented or delayed at 16 national parks in California: Cabrillo National Monument, Channel Islands National Park, Death Valley National Park, Eugene O'Neill National Historic Site, Fort Point National Historic Site, Golden Gate National Recreation Area, Lassen Volcanic National Park, Manzanar National Historic Site, Point Reyes National Seashore, Redwood National Park, San Francisco Maritime National Historical Park, Santa Monica Mountains National Recreation Area, Sequoia and Kings Canyon National Park, Whiskeytown National Recreation Area, Yosemite National Park, and Mojave National Preserve.

Balances Only with Gimmicks and Deep Cuts to Programs that Serve the Most Vulnerable and Help Expand Opportunity. On top of their cuts to middle-class investments and the ACA, the Republican budgets would cut:

- **Pell Grants:** Republican reductions to Pell would reduce financial aid for the 1,027,000 California students who rely on Pell grants to afford college.
- **Medicaid:** The House Republican proposal to block grant Medicaid would cut Federal funding to California by approximately $119.2 billion over ten years, impacting children, seniors, and people with disabilities who rely on Medicaid.
- **Supplemental Nutrition Assistance Program (SNAP):** House Republican proposals to block grant and slash SNAP would cut nutrition aid in California by an estimated $11.8 billion over a five year period (2021-2025), jeopardizing nutrition assistance for the 4,350,000 California residents who receive SNAP to help them put food on the table.

Fails to Address Our Crumbling Infrastructure: Republican budgets lack a real plan to address the looming expiration and insolvency of the Highway Trust Fund. Through the Highway Trust Fund, in FY 2014 the Federal Government obligated $3.8 billion to California through the Federal Aid Highways program for highway planning and construction and over $787.7 million through Transit Formula Grants that support our Nation's mass transit systems.

i. Numbers are rounded. For a description of how impacts were calculated, see http://go.wh.gov/RoNU1j

THE WHITE HOUSE
Office of the Press Secretary

FOR IMMEDIATE RELEASE
March 24, 2015

FACT SHEET: Republican Budget Resolutions: Same Failed Top-Down Economics for Colorado

With more than 12 million private-sector jobs created over the last 60 months, it is clear that the President's middle class economic agenda is working. But instead of taking the steps we need to strengthen the standing of working families, the Republican budgets for fiscal year (FY) 2016 would return our economy to the same top-down economics that has failed us before: cutting taxes for millionaires and billionaires, while slashing investments in the middle class that we need to grow the economy, like education, job training, and manufacturing. The Republican proposals stand in stark contrast to the President's FY 2016 Budget, which would bring middle class economics into the 21st Century. A state-by-state breakdown of this contrast, including how the Republican budgets affect Colorado, can be found in a report released today here: http://go.wh.gov/RoNU1j.

The President's Budget builds on the progress we've made and shows what we can do if we invest in America's future and commit to an economy that rewards hard work, generates rising incomes, and allows everyone to share in the prosperity of a growing America. It lays out a strategy to strengthen our middle class and help America's hard-working families get ahead in a time of relentless economic and technological change. And it makes the critical investments needed to accelerate and sustain economic growth in the long run, including in research, education, training, and infrastructure.

Republicans have chosen different priorities. Yet again, they are seeking to balance the budget on the backs of the middle class, while cutting taxes for the wealthy and well-connected. They still won't say where many of their spending cuts come from. But they are clear that their budgets would continue the harmful cuts known as sequestration in 2016, threatening economic growth, cutting programs middle-class families count on, and attempting to fund national security through irresponsible budget gimmicks. Their budgets slash domestic investments that support the middle-class even more significantly after 2016, along with programs that serve the most vulnerable Americans. House Republicans would end Medicare as we know it, transforming it from a guarantee seniors can count on into a voucher program. After five years of the Affordable Care Act, more than 16 million people have gained coverage. Yet once again, the Republican budgets propose to repeal the Affordable Care Act's coverage expansions.

The choice could not be more clear or the consequences more stark. Thanks to President Obama and the resilience of the American people, the economy is growing

again. The Republican budgets would put that growth at risk and limit opportunity for the middle-class and those seeking to join it.

In Colorado, the Republican budgets would[i]:

Cut Taxes for Millionaires and Raise Taxes for Working Families and Students: While claiming to prioritize fiscal responsibility, the Republican budgets would not ask the wealthy to contribute a single dollar to deficit reduction, and the proposals specified in the House budget would cut taxes for millionaires by an average of at least $50,000. Meanwhile, the Republican budgets do nothing to prevent tax increases averaging $1,100 for 12 million families and students paying for college and $900 for 16 million working families with children. In 2015, 223,000 Colorado families will receive a total of $200 million in tax cuts from improvements to pro-work tax credits that would expire after 2017 under the Republican budgets.

Eliminate Affordable Health Care: The Affordable Care Act is working. After five years of the Affordable Care Act, more than 16 million people have gained coverage. Yet once again, the Republican budgets propose to repeal the Affordable Care Act's coverage expansions, taking away health insurance from millions of people. In particular, the Republican budgets would eliminate coverage for 140,000 Colorado residents who have newly signed up for coverage or re-enrolled through the Marketplaces. Some of these individuals would become uninsured while others would end up with worse or less affordable coverage.

Raise Health Care Costs for Seniors: 58,800 Colorado seniors and people with disabilities benefited by an average of $880 from the closure of the Medicare Part D prescription drug donut hole in 2014 alone. Under the Republican plan to repeal the Affordable Care Act, at least that many would likely have to pay more for needed medications in future years. The House budget would also end Medicare as we know it, replacing guaranteed access to the traditional Medicare program with a voucher program, risking a death spiral in traditional Medicare.

Slash Investments in the Middle Class: Under the Republican budgets, both non-defense and base defense discretionary funding in 2016 would be at the lowest real levels in a decade. Compared to the President's Budget, if the Republican budgets were to take effect, these are just some of the impacts on Colorado:

- **Head Start:** 380 fewer children in Colorado would have access to Head Start services, representing a permanently missed opportunity to help these children enter elementary school ready to succeed.
- **Teachers and Schools:** Colorado would receive $12.3 million less funding for disadvantaged students, an amount that is enough to fund about 50 schools, 170 teacher and aide jobs, and 16,000 students.

- **Education for Children with Disabilities:** Colorado would receive $4.6 million less funding to provide educational opportunities for students with disabilities, representing an approximately 2.9 percent cut and shifting the burden for meeting these children's needs to Colorado and its local communities.
- **Job Training and Employment Services:** 36,200 fewer Colorado residents would receive job training and employment services, including help finding jobs and skills training.
- **Affordable Housing**: Colorado would receive approximately $22.4 million less in Federal funding, resulting in 1,890 fewer families receiving Housing Choice Vouchers, which enable very low-income families to afford decent, safe, and sanitary housing in the private market.
- **National Parks:** Construction and renovation projects would be prevented or delayed at seven national parks in Colorado: Bent's Old Fort National Historic Site, Curecanti National Recreation Area, Dinosaur National Monument, Florissant Fossil Beds National Monument, Great Sand Dunes National Park and Preserve, Mesa Verde National Park, and Rocky Mountain National Park.

Balances Only with Gimmicks and Deep Cuts to Programs that Serve the Most Vulnerable and Help Expand Opportunity. On top of their cuts to middle-class investments and the ACA, the Republican budgets would cut:

- **Pell Grants:** Republican reductions to Pell would reduce financial aid for the 133,000 Colorado students who rely on Pell grants to afford college.
- **Medicaid:** The House Republican proposal to block grant Medicaid would cut Federal funding to Colorado by approximately $11.0 billion over ten years, impacting children, seniors, and people with disabilities who rely on Medicaid.
- **Supplemental Nutrition Assistance Program (SNAP):** House Republican proposals to block grant and slash SNAP would cut nutrition aid in Colorado by an estimated $1.2 billion over a five year period (2021-2025), jeopardizing nutrition assistance for the 505,000 Colorado residents who receive SNAP to help them put food on the table.

Fails to Address Our Crumbling Infrastructure: Republican budgets lack a real plan to address the looming expiration and insolvency of the Highway Trust Fund. Through the Highway Trust Fund, in FY 2014 the Federal Government obligated $706.7 million to Colorado through the Federal Aid Highways program for highway planning and construction and over $144.8 million through Transit Formula Grants that support our Nation's mass transit systems.

###

i. Numbers are rounded. For a description of how impacts were calculated, see http://go.wh.gov/RoNU1

THE WHITE HOUSE
Office of the Press Secretary

FOR IMMEDIATE RELEASE
March 24, 2015

FACT SHEET: Republican Budget Resolutions: Same Failed Top-Down Economics for Connecticut

With more than 12 million private-sector jobs created over the last 60 months, it is clear that the President's middle class economic agenda is working. But instead of taking the steps we need to strengthen the standing of working families, the Republican budgets for fiscal year (FY) 2016 would return our economy to the same top-down economics that has failed us before: cutting taxes for millionaires and billionaires, while slashing investments in the middle class that we need to grow the economy, like education, job training, and manufacturing. The Republican proposals stand in stark contrast to the President's FY 2016 Budget, which would bring middle class economics into the 21st Century. A state-by-state breakdown of this contrast, including how the Republican budgets affect Connecticut, can be found in a report released today here: http://go.wh.gov/RoNU1j.

The President's Budget builds on the progress we've made and shows what we can do if we invest in America's future and commit to an economy that rewards hard work, generates rising incomes, and allows everyone to share in the prosperity of a growing America. It lays out a strategy to strengthen our middle class and help America's hard-working families get ahead in a time of relentless economic and technological change. And it makes the critical investments needed to accelerate and sustain economic growth in the long run, including in research, education, training, and infrastructure.

Republicans have chosen different priorities. Yet again, they are seeking to balance the budget on the backs of the middle class, while cutting taxes for the wealthy and well-connected. They still won't say where many of their spending cuts come from. But they are clear that their budgets would continue the harmful cuts known as sequestration in 2016, threatening economic growth, cutting programs middle-class families count on, and attempting to fund national security through irresponsible budget gimmicks. Their budgets slash domestic investments that support the middle-class even more significantly after 2016, along with programs that serve the most vulnerable Americans. House Republicans would end Medicare as we know it, transforming it from a guarantee seniors can count on into a voucher program. After five years of the Affordable Care Act, more than 16 million people have gained coverage. Yet once again, the Republican budgets propose to repeal the Affordable Care Act's coverage expansions.

The choice could not be more clear or the consequences more stark. Thanks to President Obama and the resilience of the American people, the economy is growing

again. The Republican budgets would put that growth at risk and limit opportunity for the middle-class and those seeking to join it.

In Connecticut, the Republican budgets would[i]:

Cut Taxes for Millionaires and Raise Taxes for Working Families and Students: While claiming to prioritize fiscal responsibility, the Republican budgets would not ask the wealthy to contribute a single dollar to deficit reduction, and the proposals specified in the House budget would cut taxes for millionaires by an average of at least $50,000. Meanwhile, the Republican budgets do nothing to prevent tax increases averaging $1,100 for 12 million families and students paying for college and $900 for 16 million working families with children. In 2015, 113,000 Connecticut families will receive a total of $98 million in tax cuts from improvements to pro-work tax credits that would expire after 2017 under the Republican budgets.

Eliminate Affordable Health Care: The Affordable Care Act is working. After five years of the Affordable Care Act, more than 16 million people have gained coverage. Yet once again, the Republican budgets propose to repeal the Affordable Care Act's coverage expansions, taking away health insurance from millions of people. In particular, the Republican budgets would eliminate coverage for 110,000 Connecticut residents who have newly signed up for coverage or re-enrolled through the Marketplaces. Some of these individuals would become uninsured while others would end up with worse or less affordable coverage.

Raise Health Care Costs for Seniors: 60,600 Connecticut seniors and people with disabilities benefited by an average of $1,070 from the closure of the Medicare Part D prescription drug donut hole in 2014 alone. Under the Republican plan to repeal the Affordable Care Act, at least that many would likely have to pay more for needed medications in future years. The House budget would also end Medicare as we know it, replacing guaranteed access to the traditional Medicare program with a voucher program, risking a death spiral in traditional Medicare.

Slash Investments in the Middle Class: Under the Republican budgets, both non-defense and base defense discretionary funding in 2016 would be at the lowest real levels in a decade. Compared to the President's Budget, if the Republican budgets were to take effect, these are just some of the impacts on Connecticut:

- **Head Start:** 290 fewer children in Connecticut would have access to Head Start services, representing a permanently missed opportunity to help these children enter elementary school ready to succeed.
- **Teachers and Schools:** Connecticut would receive $9.4 million less funding for disadvantaged students, an amount that is enough to fund about 40 schools, 130 teacher and aide jobs, and 9,000 students.

- **Education for Children with Disabilities:** Connecticut would receive $3.7 million less funding to provide educational opportunities for students with disabilities, representing an approximately 2.8 percent cut and shifting the burden for meeting these children's needs to Connecticut and its local communities.
- **Job Training and Employment Services:** 25,800 fewer Connecticut residents would receive job training and employment services, including help finding jobs and skills training.
- **Affordable Housing**: Connecticut would receive approximately $34.9 million less in Federal funding, resulting in 2,190 fewer families receiving Housing Choice Vouchers, which enable very low-income families to afford decent, safe, and sanitary housing in the private market.

Balances Only with Gimmicks and Deep Cuts to Programs that Serve the Most Vulnerable and Help Expand Opportunity. On top of their cuts to middle-class investments and the ACA, the Republican budgets would cut:

- **Pell Grants:** Republican reductions to Pell would reduce financial aid for the 71,000 Connecticut students who rely on Pell grants to afford college.
- **Medicaid:** The House Republican proposal to block grant Medicaid would cut Federal funding to Connecticut by approximately $12.7 billion over ten years, impacting children, seniors, and people with disabilities who rely on Medicaid.
- **Supplemental Nutrition Assistance Program (SNAP):** House Republican proposals to block grant and slash SNAP would cut nutrition aid in Connecticut by an estimated $1.1 billion over a five year period (2021-2025), jeopardizing nutrition assistance for the 439,000 Connecticut residents who receive SNAP to help them put food on the table.

Fails to Address Our Crumbling Infrastructure: Republican budgets lack a real plan to address the looming expiration and insolvency of the Highway Trust Fund. Through the Highway Trust Fund, in FY 2014 the Federal Government obligated $476.2 million to Connecticut through the Federal Aid Highways program for highway planning and construction and over $327.9 million through Transit Formula Grants that support our Nation's mass transit systems.

###

i. Numbers are rounded. For a description of how impacts were calculated, see http://go.wh.gov/RoNU1j

FOR IMMEDIATE RELEASE
March 24, 2015

FACT SHEET: Republican Budget Resolutions: Same Failed Top-Down Economics for Delaware

With more than 12 million private-sector jobs created over the last 60 months, it is clear that the President's middle class economic agenda is working. But instead of taking the steps we need to strengthen the standing of working families, the Republican budgets for fiscal year (FY) 2016 would return our economy to the same top-down economics that has failed us before: cutting taxes for millionaires and billionaires, while slashing investments in the middle class that we need to grow the economy, like education, job training, and manufacturing. The Republican proposals stand in stark contrast to the President's FY 2016 Budget, which would bring middle class economics into the 21st Century. A state-by-state breakdown of this contrast, including how the Republican budgets affect Delaware, can be found in a report released today here: http://go.wh.gov/RoNU1j.

The President's Budget builds on the progress we've made and shows what we can do if we invest in America's future and commit to an economy that rewards hard work, generates rising incomes, and allows everyone to share in the prosperity of a growing America. It lays out a strategy to strengthen our middle class and help America's hard-working families get ahead in a time of relentless economic and technological change. And it makes the critical investments needed to accelerate and sustain economic growth in the long run, including in research, education, training, and infrastructure.

Republicans have chosen different priorities. Yet again, they are seeking to balance the budget on the backs of the middle class, while cutting taxes for the wealthy and well-connected. They still won't say where many of their spending cuts come from. But they are clear that their budgets would continue the harmful cuts known as sequestration in 2016, threatening economic growth, cutting programs middle-class families count on, and attempting to fund national security through irresponsible budget gimmicks. Their budgets slash domestic investments that support the middle-class even more significantly after 2016, along with programs that serve the most vulnerable Americans. House Republicans would end Medicare as we know it, transforming it from a guarantee seniors can count on into a voucher program. After five years of the Affordable Care Act, more than 16 million people have gained coverage. Yet once again, the Republican budgets propose to repeal the Affordable Care Act's coverage expansions.

The choice could not be more clear or the consequences more stark. Thanks to President Obama and the resilience of the American people, the economy is growing

again. The Republican budgets would put that growth at risk and limit opportunity for the middle-class and those seeking to join it.

In Delaware, the Republican budgets would[i]:

Cut Taxes for Millionaires and Raise Taxes for Working Families and Students:
While claiming to prioritize fiscal responsibility, the Republican budgets would not ask the wealthy to contribute a single dollar to deficit reduction, and the proposals specified in the House budget would cut taxes for millionaires by an average of at least $50,000. Meanwhile, the Republican budgets do nothing to prevent tax increases averaging $1,100 for 12 million families and students paying for college and $900 for 16 million working families with children. In 2015, 39,000 Delaware families will receive a total of $35 million in tax cuts from improvements to pro-work tax credits that would expire after 2017 under the Republican budgets.

Eliminate Affordable Health Care: The Affordable Care Act is working. After five years of the Affordable Care Act, more than 16 million people have gained coverage. Yet once again, the Republican budgets propose to repeal the Affordable Care Act's coverage expansions, taking away health insurance from millions of people. In particular, the Republican budgets would eliminate coverage for 25,000 Delaware residents who have newly signed up for coverage or re-enrolled through the Marketplaces. Some of these individuals would become uninsured while others would end up with worse or less affordable coverage.

Raise Health Care Costs for Seniors: 23,900 Delaware seniors and people with disabilities benefited by an average of $1,090 from the closure of the Medicare Part D prescription drug donut hole in 2014 alone. Under the Republican plan to repeal the Affordable Care Act, at least that many would likely have to pay more for needed medications in future years. The House budget would also end Medicare as we know it, replacing guaranteed access to the traditional Medicare program with a voucher program, risking a death spiral in traditional Medicare.

Slash Investments in the Middle Class: Under the Republican budgets, both non-defense and base defense discretionary funding in 2016 would be at the lowest real levels in a decade. Compared to the President's Budget, if the Republican budgets were to take effect, these are just some of the impacts on Delaware:

- **Head Start:** 70 fewer children in Delaware would have access to Head Start services, representing a permanently missed opportunity to help these children enter elementary school ready to succeed.
- **Teachers and Schools:** Delaware would receive $4.1 million less funding for disadvantaged students, an amount that is enough to fund about 10 schools, 60 teacher and aide jobs, and 7,000 students.

- **Education for Children with Disabilities:** Delaware would receive $1.3 million less funding to provide educational opportunities for students with disabilities, representing an approximately 3.6 percent cut and shifting the burden for meeting these children's needs to Delaware and its local communities.
- **Job Training and Employment Services:** 6,300 fewer Delaware residents would receive job training and employment services, including help finding jobs and skills training.
- **Affordable Housing**: Delaware would receive approximately $3.9 million less in Federal funding, resulting in 300 fewer families receiving Housing Choice Vouchers, which enable very low-income families to afford decent, safe, and sanitary housing in the private market.

Balances Only with Gimmicks and Deep Cuts to Programs that Serve the Most Vulnerable and Help Expand Opportunity. On top of their cuts to middle-class investments and the ACA, the Republican budgets would cut:

- **Pell Grants:** Republican reductions to Pell would reduce financial aid for the 16,000 Delaware students who rely on Pell grants to afford college.
- **Medicaid:** The House Republican proposal to block grant Medicaid would cut Federal funding to Delaware by approximately $3.4 billion over ten years, impacting children, seniors, and people with disabilities who rely on Medicaid.
- **Supplemental Nutrition Assistance Program (SNAP):** House Republican proposals to block grant and slash SNAP would cut nutrition aid in Delaware by an estimated $300 million over a five year period (2021-2025), jeopardizing nutrition assistance for the 150,000 Delaware residents who receive SNAP to help them put food on the table.

Fails to Address Our Crumbling Infrastructure: Republican budgets lack a real plan to address the looming expiration and insolvency of the Highway Trust Fund. Through the Highway Trust Fund, in FY 2014 the Federal Government obligated $206.9 million to Delaware through the Federal Aid Highways program for highway planning and construction and over $19.3 million through Transit Formula Grants that support our Nation's mass transit systems.

i. Numbers are rounded. For a description of how impacts were calculated, see http://go.wh.gov/RoNU1j

THE WHITE HOUSE
Office of the Press Secretary

FOR IMMEDIATE RELEASE
March 24, 2015

FACT SHEET: Republican Budget Resolutions: Same Failed Top-Down Economics for the District of Columbia

With more than 12 million private-sector jobs created over the last 60 months, it is clear that the President's middle class economic agenda is working. But instead of taking the steps we need to strengthen the standing of working families, the Republican budgets for fiscal year (FY) 2016 would return our economy to the same top-down economics that has failed us before: cutting taxes for millionaires and billionaires, while slashing investments in the middle class that we need to grow the economy, like education, job training, and manufacturing. The Republican proposals stand in stark contrast to the President's FY 2016 Budget, which would bring middle class economics into the 21st Century. A state-by-state breakdown of this contrast, including how the Republican budgets affect the District of Columbia, can be found in a report released today here: http://go.wh.gov/RoNU1j.

The President's Budget builds on the progress we've made and shows what we can do if we invest in America's future and commit to an economy that rewards hard work, generates rising incomes, and allows everyone to share in the prosperity of a growing America. It lays out a strategy to strengthen our middle class and help America's hard-working families get ahead in a time of relentless economic and technological change. And it makes the critical investments needed to accelerate and sustain economic growth in the long run, including in research, education, training, and infrastructure.

Republicans have chosen different priorities. Yet again, they are seeking to balance the budget on the backs of the middle class, while cutting taxes for the wealthy and well-connected. They still won't say where many of their spending cuts come from. But they are clear that their budgets would continue the harmful cuts known as sequestration in 2016, threatening economic growth, cutting programs middle-class families count on, and attempting to fund national security through irresponsible budget gimmicks. Their budgets slash domestic investments that support the middle-class even more significantly after 2016, along with programs that serve the most vulnerable Americans. House Republicans would end Medicare as we know it, transforming it from a guarantee seniors can count on into a voucher program. After five years of the Affordable Care Act, more than 16 million people have gained coverage. Yet once again, the Republican budgets propose to repeal the Affordable Care Act's coverage expansions.

The choice could not be more clear or the consequences more stark. Thanks to President Obama and the resilience of the American people, the economy is growing

again. The Republican budgets would put that growth at risk and limit opportunity for the middle-class and those seeking to join it.

In the District of Columbia, the Republican budgets would[i]:

Cut Taxes for Millionaires and Raise Taxes for Working Families and Students: While claiming to prioritize fiscal responsibility, the Republican budgets would not ask the wealthy to contribute a single dollar to deficit reduction, and the proposals specified in the House budget would cut taxes for millionaires by an average of at least $50,000. Meanwhile, the Republican budgets do nothing to prevent tax increases averaging $1,100 for 12 million families and students paying for college and $900 for 16 million working families with children. In 2015, 24,000 District of Columbia families will receive a total of $23 million in tax cuts from improvements to pro-work tax credits that would expire after 2017 under the Republican budgets.

Eliminate Affordable Health Care: The Affordable Care Act is working. After five years of the Affordable Care Act, more than 16 million people have gained coverage. Yet once again, the Republican budgets propose to repeal the Affordable Care Act's coverage expansions, taking away health insurance from millions of people. In particular, the Republican budgets would eliminate coverage for 18,000 District of Columbia residents who have newly signed up for coverage or re-enrolled through the Marketplaces. Some of these individuals would become uninsured while others would end up with worse or less affordable coverage.

Raise Health Care Costs for Seniors: 3,200 District of Columbia seniors and people with disabilities benefited by an average of $960 from the closure of the Medicare Part D prescription drug donut hole in 2014 alone. Under the Republican plan to repeal the Affordable Care Act, at least that many would likely have to pay more for needed medications in future years. The House budget would also end Medicare as we know it, replacing guaranteed access to the traditional Medicare program with a voucher program, risking a death spiral in traditional Medicare.

Slash Investments in the Middle Class: Under the Republican budgets, both non-defense and base defense discretionary funding in 2016 would be at the lowest real levels in a decade. Compared to the President's Budget, if the Republican budgets were to take effect, these are just some of the impacts on the District of Columbia:

- **Head Start:** 130 fewer children in the District of Columbia would have access to Head Start services, representing a permanently missed opportunity to help these children enter elementary school ready to succeed.
- **Teachers and Schools:** The District of Columbia would receive $3.9 million less funding for disadvantaged students, an amount that is enough to fund about 20 schools, 50 teacher and aide jobs, and 6,000 students.

- **Education for Children with Disabilities:** The District of Columbia would receive $800,000 less funding to provide educational opportunities for students with disabilities, representing an approximately 4.5 percent cut and shifting the burden for meeting these children's needs to the District of Columbia and its local communities.
- **Job Training and Employment Services:** 7,100 fewer District of Columbia residents would receive job training and employment services, including help finding jobs and skills training.
- **Affordable Housing:** The District of Columbia would receive approximately $18.0 million less in Federal funding, resulting in 670 fewer families receiving Housing Choice Vouchers, which enable very low-income families to afford decent, safe, and sanitary housing in the private market.
- **National Parks:** Construction and renovation projects would be prevented or delayed at three national parks in the District of Columbia: National Capital Parks-East, The White House, and National Mall and Memorial Parks.

Balances Only with Gimmicks and Deep Cuts to Programs that Serve the Most Vulnerable and Help Expand Opportunity. On top of their cuts to middle-class investments and the ACA, the Republican budgets would cut:

- **Pell Grants:** Republican reductions to Pell would reduce financial aid for the 38,000 District of Columbia students who rely on Pell grants to afford college.
- **Medicaid:** The House Republican proposal to block grant Medicaid would cut Federal funding to the District of Columbia by approximately $5.6 billion over ten years, impacting children, seniors, and people with disabilities who rely on Medicaid.
- **Supplemental Nutrition Assistance Program (SNAP):** House Republican proposals to block grant and slash SNAP would cut nutrition aid in the District of Columbia by an estimated $400 million over a five year period (2021-2025), jeopardizing nutrition assistance for the 143,000 District of Columbia residents who receive SNAP to help them put food on the table.

Fails to Address Our Crumbling Infrastructure: Republican budgets lack a real plan to address the looming expiration and insolvency of the Highway Trust Fund. Through the Highway Trust Fund, in FY 2014 the Federal Government obligated $152.7 million to the District of Columbia through the Federal Aid Highways program for highway planning and construction and over $295.8 million through Transit Formula Grants that support our Nation's mass transit systems.

###

i. Numbers are rounded. For a description of how impacts were calculated, see http://go.wh.gov/RoNU1j

THE WHITE HOUSE
Office of the Press Secretary

FOR IMMEDIATE RELEASE
March 24, 2015

FACT SHEET: Republican Budget Resolutions: Same Failed Top-Down Economics for Florida

With more than 12 million private-sector jobs created over the last 60 months, it is clear that the President's middle class economic agenda is working. But instead of taking the steps we need to strengthen the standing of working families, the Republican budgets for fiscal year (FY) 2016 would return our economy to the same top-down economics that has failed us before: cutting taxes for millionaires and billionaires, while slashing investments in the middle class that we need to grow the economy, like education, job training, and manufacturing. The Republican proposals stand in stark contrast to the President's FY 2016 Budget, which would bring middle class economics into the 21st Century. A state-by-state breakdown of this contrast, including how the Republican budgets affect Florida, can be found in a report released today here: http://go.wh.gov/RoNU1j.

The President's Budget builds on the progress we've made and shows what we can do if we invest in America's future and commit to an economy that rewards hard work, generates rising incomes, and allows everyone to share in the prosperity of a growing America. It lays out a strategy to strengthen our middle class and help America's hard-working families get ahead in a time of relentless economic and technological change. And it makes the critical investments needed to accelerate and sustain economic growth in the long run, including in research, education, training, and infrastructure.

Republicans have chosen different priorities. Yet again, they are seeking to balance the budget on the backs of the middle class, while cutting taxes for the wealthy and well-connected. They still won't say where many of their spending cuts come from. But they are clear that their budgets would continue the harmful cuts known as sequestration in 2016, threatening economic growth, cutting programs middle-class families count on, and attempting to fund national security through irresponsible budget gimmicks. Their budgets slash domestic investments that support the middle-class even more significantly after 2016, along with programs that serve the most vulnerable Americans. House Republicans would end Medicare as we know it, transforming it from a guarantee seniors can count on into a voucher program. After five years of the Affordable Care Act, more than 16 million people have gained coverage. Yet once again, the Republican budgets propose to repeal the Affordable Care Act's coverage expansions.

The choice could not be more clear or the consequences more stark. Thanks to President Obama and the resilience of the American people, the economy is growing

again. The Republican budgets would put that growth at risk and limit opportunity for the middle-class and those seeking to join it.

In Florida, the Republican budgets would[i]:

Cut Taxes for Millionaires and Raise Taxes for Working Families and Students: While claiming to prioritize fiscal responsibility, the Republican budgets would not ask the wealthy to contribute a single dollar to deficit reduction, and the proposals specified in the House budget would cut taxes for millionaires by an average of at least $50,000. Meanwhile, the Republican budgets do nothing to prevent tax increases averaging $1,100 for 12 million families and students paying for college and $900 for 16 million working families with children. In 2015, nearly 1.1 million Florida families will receive a total of $965 million in tax cuts from improvements to pro-work tax credits that would expire after 2017 under the Republican budgets.

Eliminate Affordable Health Care: The Affordable Care Act is working. After five years of the Affordable Care Act, more than 16 million people have gained coverage. Yet once again, the Republican budgets propose to repeal the Affordable Care Act's coverage expansions, taking away health insurance from millions of people. In particular, the Republican budgets would eliminate coverage for nearly 1.6 million Florida residents who have newly signed up for coverage or re-enrolled through the Marketplaces. Some of these individuals would become uninsured while others would end up with worse or less affordable coverage.

Raise Health Care Costs for Seniors: 346,100 Florida seniors and people with disabilities benefited by an average of $880 from the closure of the Medicare Part D prescription drug donut hole in 2014 alone. Under the Republican plan to repeal the Affordable Care Act, at least that many would likely have to pay more for needed medications in future years. The House budget would also end Medicare as we know it, replacing guaranteed access to the traditional Medicare program with a voucher program, risking a death spiral in traditional Medicare.

Slash Investments in the Middle Class: Under the Republican budgets, both non-defense and base defense discretionary funding in 2016 would be at the lowest real levels in a decade. Compared to the President's Budget, if the Republican budgets were to take effect, these are just some of the impacts on Florida:

- **Head Start:** 1,460 fewer children in Florida would have access to Head Start services, representing a permanently missed opportunity to help these children enter elementary school ready to succeed.
- **Teachers and Schools:** Florida would receive $74.5 million less funding for disadvantaged students, an amount that is enough to fund about 160 schools, 1,020 teacher and aide jobs, and 113,000 students.

- **Education for Children with Disabilities:** Florida would receive $18.3 million less funding to provide educational opportunities for students with disabilities, representing an approximately 2.8 percent cut and shifting the burden for meeting these children's needs to Florida and its local communities.
- **Job Training and Employment Services:** 130,500 fewer Florida residents would receive job training and employment services, including help finding jobs and skills training.
- **Affordable Housing:** Florida would receive approximately $80.2 million less in Federal funding, resulting in 5,990 fewer families receiving Housing Choice Vouchers, which enable very low-income families to afford decent, safe, and sanitary housing in the private market.
- **National Parks:** Construction and renovation projects would be prevented or delayed at two national parks in Florida: Biscayne National Park and Castillo De San Marcos National Monument.

Balances Only with Gimmicks and Deep Cuts to Programs that Serve the Most Vulnerable and Help Expand Opportunity. On top of their cuts to middle-class investments and the ACA, the Republican budgets would cut:

- **Pell Grants:** Republican reductions to Pell would reduce financial aid for the 572,000 Florida students who rely on Pell grants to afford college.
- **Medicaid:** The House Republican proposal to block grant Medicaid would cut Federal funding to Florida by approximately $38.7 billion over ten years, impacting children, seniors, and people with disabilities who rely on Medicaid.
- **Supplemental Nutrition Assistance Program (SNAP):** House Republican proposals to block grant and slash SNAP would cut nutrition aid in Florida by an estimated $8.7 billion over a five year period (2021-2025), jeopardizing nutrition assistance for the 3,526,000 Florida residents who receive SNAP to help them put food on the table.

Fails to Address Our Crumbling Infrastructure: Republican budgets lack a real plan to address the looming expiration and insolvency of the Highway Trust Fund. Through the Highway Trust Fund, in FY 2014 the Federal Government obligated $1.8 billion to Florida through the Federal Aid Highways program for highway planning and construction and over $321.7 million through Transit Formula Grants that support our Nation's mass transit systems.

i. Numbers are rounded. For a description of how impacts were calculated, see http://go.wh.gov/RoNU1j

THE WHITE HOUSE
Office of the Press Secretary

FOR IMMEDIATE RELEASE
March 24, 2015

FACT SHEET: Republican Budget Resolutions: Same Failed Top-Down Economics for Georgia

With more than 12 million private-sector jobs created over the last 60 months, it is clear that the President's middle class economic agenda is working. But instead of taking the steps we need to strengthen the standing of working families, the Republican budgets for fiscal year (FY) 2016 would return our economy to the same top-down economics that has failed us before: cutting taxes for millionaires and billionaires, while slashing investments in the middle class that we need to grow the economy, like education, job training, and manufacturing. The Republican proposals stand in stark contrast to the President's FY 2016 Budget, which would bring middle class economics into the 21st Century. A state-by-state breakdown of this contrast, including how the Republican budgets affect Georgia, can be found in a report released today here: http://go.wh.gov/RoNU1j.

The President's Budget builds on the progress we've made and shows what we can do if we invest in America's future and commit to an economy that rewards hard work, generates rising incomes, and allows everyone to share in the prosperity of a growing America. It lays out a strategy to strengthen our middle class and help America's hard-working families get ahead in a time of relentless economic and technological change. And it makes the critical investments needed to accelerate and sustain economic growth in the long run, including in research, education, training, and infrastructure.

Republicans have chosen different priorities. Yet again, they are seeking to balance the budget on the backs of the middle class, while cutting taxes for the wealthy and well-connected. They still won't say where many of their spending cuts come from. But they are clear that their budgets would continue the harmful cuts known as sequestration in 2016, threatening economic growth, cutting programs middle-class families count on, and attempting to fund national security through irresponsible budget gimmicks. Their budgets slash domestic investments that support the middle-class even more significantly after 2016, along with programs that serve the most vulnerable Americans. House Republicans would end Medicare as we know it, transforming it from a guarantee seniors can count on into a voucher program. After five years of the Affordable Care Act, more than 16 million people have gained coverage. Yet once again, the Republican budgets propose to repeal the Affordable Care Act's coverage expansions.

The choice could not be more clear or the consequences more stark. Thanks to President Obama and the resilience of the American people, the economy is growing

again. The Republican budgets would put that growth at risk and limit opportunity for the middle-class and those seeking to join it.

In Georgia, the Republican budgets would[i]:

Cut Taxes for Millionaires and Raise Taxes for Working Families and Students: While claiming to prioritize fiscal responsibility, the Republican budgets would not ask the wealthy to contribute a single dollar to deficit reduction, and the proposals specified in the House budget would cut taxes for millionaires by an average of at least $50,000. Meanwhile, the Republican budgets do nothing to prevent tax increases averaging $1,100 for 12 million families and students paying for college and $900 for 16 million working families with children. In 2015, 642,000 Georgia families will receive a total of $601 million in tax cuts from improvements to pro-work tax credits that would expire after 2017 under the Republican budgets.

Eliminate Affordable Health Care: The Affordable Care Act is working. After five years of the Affordable Care Act, more than 16 million people have gained coverage. Yet once again, the Republican budgets propose to repeal the Affordable Care Act's coverage expansions, taking away health insurance from millions of people. In particular, the Republican budgets would eliminate coverage for 541,000 Georgia residents who have newly signed up for coverage or re-enrolled through the Marketplaces. Some of these individuals would become uninsured while others would end up with worse or less affordable coverage.

Raise Health Care Costs for Seniors: 141,600 Georgia seniors and people with disabilities benefited by an average of $930 from the closure of the Medicare Part D prescription drug donut hole in 2014 alone. Under the Republican plan to repeal the Affordable Care Act, at least that many would likely have to pay more for needed medications in future years. The House budget would also end Medicare as we know it, replacing guaranteed access to the traditional Medicare program with a voucher program, risking a death spiral in traditional Medicare.

Slash Investments in the Middle Class: Under the Republican budgets, both non-defense and base defense discretionary funding in 2016 would be at the lowest real levels in a decade. Compared to the President's Budget, if the Republican budgets were to take effect, these are just some of the impacts on Georgia:

- **Head Start:** 940 fewer children in Georgia would have access to Head Start services, representing a permanently missed opportunity to help these children enter elementary school ready to succeed.
- **Teachers and Schools:** Georgia would receive $41.9 million less funding for disadvantaged students, an amount that is enough to fund about 130 schools, 580 teacher and aide jobs, and 80,000 students.

- **Education for Children with Disabilities:** Georgia would receive $15.3 million less funding to provide educational opportunities for students with disabilities, representing an approximately 4.5 percent cut and shifting the burden for meeting these children's needs to Georgia and its local communities.
- **Job Training and Employment Services:** 67,500 fewer Georgia residents would receive job training and employment services, including help finding jobs and skills training.
- **Affordable Housing**: Georgia would receive approximately $46.2 million less in Federal funding, resulting in 3,250 fewer families receiving Housing Choice Vouchers, which enable very low-income families to afford decent, safe, and sanitary housing in the private market.
- **National Parks:** Construction and renovation projects would be prevented or delayed at four national parks in Georgia: Chattahoochee River National Recreation Area, Kennesaw Mountain National Battlefield Park, Appalachian National Scenic Trail, and the Martin Luther King Jr. National Historic Site.

Balances Only with Gimmicks and Deep Cuts to Programs that Serve the Most Vulnerable and Help Expand Opportunity. On top of their cuts to middle-class investments and the ACA, the Republican budgets would cut:

- **Pell Grants:** Republican reductions to Pell would reduce financial aid for the 275,000 Georgia students who rely on Pell grants to afford college.
- **Medicaid:** The House Republican proposal to block grant Medicaid would cut Federal funding to Georgia by approximately $20.6 billion over ten years, impacting children, seniors, and people with disabilities who rely on Medicaid.
- **Supplemental Nutrition Assistance Program (SNAP):** House Republican proposals to block grant and slash SNAP would cut nutrition aid in Georgia by an estimated $4.5 billion over a five year period (2021-2025), jeopardizing nutrition assistance for the 1,816,000 Georgia residents who receive SNAP to help them put food on the table.

Fails to Address Our Crumbling Infrastructure: Republican budgets lack a real plan to address the looming expiration and insolvency of the Highway Trust Fund. Through the Highway Trust Fund, in FY 2014 the Federal Government obligated $1.3 billion to Georgia through the Federal Aid Highways program for highway planning and construction and over $309.9 million through Transit Formula Grants that support our Nation's mass transit systems.

###

i. Numbers are rounded. For a description of how impacts were calculate, see http://go.wh.gov/RoNU1j

THE WHITE HOUSE
Office of the Press Secretary

FOR IMMEDIATE RELEASE
March 24, 2015

FACT SHEET: Republican Budget Resolutions: Same Failed Top-Down Economics for Hawaii

With more than 12 million private-sector jobs created over the last 60 months, it is clear that the President's middle class economic agenda is working. But instead of taking the steps we need to strengthen the standing of working families, the Republican budgets for fiscal year (FY) 2016 would return our economy to the same top-down economics that has failed us before: cutting taxes for millionaires and billionaires, while slashing investments in the middle class that we need to grow the economy, like education, job training, and manufacturing. The Republican proposals stand in stark contrast to the President's FY 2016 Budget, which would bring middle class economics into the 21st Century. A state-by-state breakdown of this contrast, including how the Republican budgets affect Hawaii, can be found in a report released today here: http://go.wh.gov/RoNU1j.

The President's Budget builds on the progress we've made and shows what we can do if we invest in America's future and commit to an economy that rewards hard work, generates rising incomes, and allows everyone to share in the prosperity of a growing America. It lays out a strategy to strengthen our middle class and help America's hard-working families get ahead in a time of relentless economic and technological change. And it makes the critical investments needed to accelerate and sustain economic growth in the long run, including in research, education, training, and infrastructure.

Republicans have chosen different priorities. Yet again, they are seeking to balance the budget on the backs of the middle class, while cutting taxes for the wealthy and well-connected. They still won't say where many of their spending cuts come from. But they are clear that their budgets would continue the harmful cuts known as sequestration in 2016, threatening economic growth, cutting programs middle-class families count on, and attempting to fund national security through irresponsible budget gimmicks. Their budgets slash domestic investments that support the middle-class even more significantly after 2016, along with programs that serve the most vulnerable Americans. House Republicans would end Medicare as we know it, transforming it from a guarantee seniors can count on into a voucher program. After five years of the Affordable Care Act, more than 16 million people have gained coverage. Yet once again, the Republican budgets propose to repeal the Affordable Care Act's coverage expansions.

The choice could not be more clear or the consequences more stark. Thanks to President Obama and the resilience of the American people, the economy is growing

again. The Republican budgets would put that growth at risk and limit opportunity for the middle-class and those seeking to join it.

In Hawaii, the Republican budgets would[i]:

Cut Taxes for Millionaires and Raise Taxes for Working Families and Students: While claiming to prioritize fiscal responsibility, the Republican budgets would not ask the wealthy to contribute a single dollar to deficit reduction, and the proposals specified in the House budget would cut taxes for millionaires by an average of at least $50,000. Meanwhile, the Republican budgets do nothing to prevent tax increases averaging $1,100 for 12 million families and students paying for college and $900 for 16 million working families with children. In 2015, 57,000 Hawaii families will receive a total of $50 million in tax cuts from improvements to pro-work tax credits that would expire after 2017 under the Republican budgets.

Eliminate Affordable Health Care: The Affordable Care Act is working. After five years of the Affordable Care Act, more than 16 million people have gained coverage. Yet once again, the Republican budgets propose to repeal the Affordable Care Act's coverage expansions, taking away health insurance from millions of people. In particular, the Republican budgets would eliminate coverage for 13,000 Hawaii residents who have newly signed up for coverage or re-enrolled through the Marketplaces. Some of these individuals would become uninsured while others would end up with worse or less affordable coverage.

Raise Health Care Costs for Seniors: 24,100 Hawaii seniors and people with disabilities benefited by an average of $1,090 from the closure of the Medicare Part D prescription drug donut hole in 2014 alone. Under the Republican plan to repeal the Affordable Care Act, at least that many would likely have to pay more for needed medications in future years. The House budget would also end Medicare as we know it, replacing guaranteed access to the traditional Medicare program with a voucher program, risking a death spiral in traditional Medicare.

Slash Investments in the Middle Class: Under the Republican budgets, both non-defense and base defense discretionary funding in 2016 would be at the lowest real levels in a decade. Compared to the President's Budget, if the Republican budgets were to take effect, these are just some of the impacts on Hawaii:

- **Head Start:** 120 fewer children in Hawaii would have access to Head Start services, representing a permanently missed opportunity to help these children enter elementary school ready to succeed.
- **Teachers and Schools:** Hawaii would receive $4.2 million less funding for disadvantaged students, an amount that is enough to fund about 20 schools, 60 teacher and aide jobs, and 11,000 students.

- **Education for Children with Disabilities:** Hawaii would receive $1.1 million less funding to provide educational opportunities for students with disabilities, representing an approximately 2.9 percent cut and shifting the burden for meeting these children's needs to Hawaii and its local communities.
- **Job Training and Employment Services:** 8,000 fewer Hawaii residents would receive job training and employment services, including help finding jobs and skills training.
- **Affordable Housing:** Hawaii would receive approximately $10.5 million less in Federal funding, resulting in 580 fewer families receiving Housing Choice Vouchers, which enable very low-income families to afford decent, safe, and sanitary housing in the private market.
- **National Parks:** Construction and renovation projects would be prevented or delayed at four national parks in Hawaii: Heleakala National Park, Hawaii Volcanoes National Park, Kalaupapa National Historical Park, and World War II Valor in The Pacific National Monument.

Balances Only with Gimmicks and Deep Cuts to Programs that Serve the Most Vulnerable and Help Expand Opportunity. On top of their cuts to middle-class investments and the ACA, the Republican budgets would cut:

- **Pell Grants:** Republican reductions to Pell would reduce financial aid for the 22,000 Hawaii students who rely on Pell grants to afford college.
- **Medicaid:** The House Republican proposal to block grant Medicaid would cut Federal funding to Hawaii by approximately $3.7 billion over ten years, impacting children, seniors, and people with disabilities who rely on Medicaid.
- **Supplemental Nutrition Assistance Program (SNAP):** House Republican proposals to block grant and slash SNAP would cut nutrition aid in Hawaii by an estimated $800 million over a five year period (2021-2025), jeopardizing nutrition assistance for the 194,000 Hawaii residents who receive SNAP to help them put food on the table.

Fails to Address Our Crumbling Infrastructure: Republican budgets lack a real plan to address the looming expiration and insolvency of the Highway Trust Fund. Through the Highway Trust Fund, in FY 2014 the Federal Government obligated $157.2 million to Hawaii through the Federal Aid Highways program for highway planning and construction and over $54.8 million through Transit Formula Grants that support our Nation's mass transit systems.

###

i. Numbers are rounded. For a description of how impacts were calculated, see http://go.wh.gov/RoNU1j

THE WHITE HOUSE
Office of the Press Secretary

FOR IMMEDIATE RELEASE
March 24, 2015

FACT SHEET: Republican Budget Resolutions: Same Failed Top-Down Economics for Idaho

With more than 12 million private-sector jobs created over the last 60 months, it is clear that the President's middle class economic agenda is working. But instead of taking the steps we need to strengthen the standing of working families, the Republican budgets for fiscal year (FY) 2016 would return our economy to the same top-down economics that has failed us before: cutting taxes for millionaires and billionaires, while slashing investments in the middle class that we need to grow the economy, like education, job training, and manufacturing. The Republican proposals stand in stark contrast to the President's FY 2016 Budget, which would bring middle class economics into the 21st Century. A state-by-state breakdown of this contrast, including how the Republican budgets affect Idaho, can be found in a report released today here: http://go.wh.gov/RoNU1j.

The President's Budget builds on the progress we've made and shows what we can do if we invest in America's future and commit to an economy that rewards hard work, generates rising incomes, and allows everyone to share in the prosperity of a growing America. It lays out a strategy to strengthen our middle class and help America's hard-working families get ahead in a time of relentless economic and technological change. And it makes the critical investments needed to accelerate and sustain economic growth in the long run, including in research, education, training, and infrastructure.

Republicans have chosen different priorities. Yet again, they are seeking to balance the budget on the backs of the middle class, while cutting taxes for the wealthy and well-connected. They still won't say where many of their spending cuts come from. But they are clear that their budgets would continue the harmful cuts known as sequestration in 2016, threatening economic growth, cutting programs middle-class families count on, and attempting to fund national security through irresponsible budget gimmicks. Their budgets slash domestic investments that support the middle-class even more significantly after 2016, along with programs that serve the most vulnerable Americans. House Republicans would end Medicare as we know it, transforming it from a guarantee seniors can count on into a voucher program. After five years of the Affordable Care Act, more than 16 million people have gained coverage. Yet once again, the Republican budgets propose to repeal the Affordable Care Act's coverage expansions.

The choice could not be more clear or the consequences more stark. Thanks to President Obama and the resilience of the American people, the economy is growing

again. The Republican budgets would put that growth at risk and limit opportunity for the middle-class and those seeking to join it.

In Idaho, the Republican budgets would[i]:

Cut Taxes for Millionaires and Raise Taxes for Working Families and Students: While claiming to prioritize fiscal responsibility, the Republican budgets would not ask the wealthy to contribute a single dollar to deficit reduction, and the proposals specified in the House budget would cut taxes for millionaires by an average of at least $50,000. Meanwhile, the Republican budgets do nothing to prevent tax increases averaging $1,100 for 12 million families and students paying for college and $900 for 16 million working families with children. In 2015, 88,000 Idaho families will receive a total of $80 million in tax cuts from improvements to pro-work tax credits that would expire after 2017 under the Republican budgets.

Eliminate Affordable Health Care: The Affordable Care Act is working. After five years of the Affordable Care Act, more than 16 million people have gained coverage. Yet once again, the Republican budgets propose to repeal the Affordable Care Act's coverage expansions, taking away health insurance from millions of people. In particular, the Republican budgets would eliminate coverage for 97,000 Idaho residents who have newly signed up for coverage or re-enrolled through the Marketplaces. Some of these individuals would become uninsured while others would end up with worse or less affordable coverage.

Raise Health Care Costs for Seniors: 18,900 Idaho seniors and people with disabilities benefited by an average of $780 from the closure of the Medicare Part D prescription drug donut hole in 2014 alone. Under the Republican plan to repeal the Affordable Care Act, at least that many would likely have to pay more for needed medications in future years. The House budget would also end Medicare as we know it, replacing guaranteed access to the traditional Medicare program with a voucher program, risking a death spiral in traditional Medicare.

Slash Investments in the Middle Class: Under the Republican budgets, both non-defense and base defense discretionary funding in 2016 would be at the lowest real levels in a decade. Compared to the President's Budget, if the Republican budgets were to take effect, these are just some of the impacts on Idaho:

- **Head Start:** 120 fewer children in Idaho would have access to Head Start services, representing a permanently missed opportunity to help these children enter elementary school ready to succeed.
- **Teachers and Schools:** Idaho would receive $4.5 million less funding for disadvantaged students, an amount that is enough to fund about 30 schools, 60 teacher and aide jobs, and 10,000 students.

- **Education for Children with Disabilities:** Idaho would receive $1.6 million less funding to provide educational opportunities for students with disabilities, representing an approximately 2.9 percent cut and shifting the burden for meeting these children's needs to Idaho and its local communities.
- **Job Training and Employment Services:** 20,400 fewer Idaho residents would receive job training and employment services, including help finding jobs and skills training.
- **Affordable Housing**: Idaho would receive approximately $3.6 million less in Federal funding, resulting in 410 fewer families receiving Housing Choice Vouchers, which enable very low-income families to afford decent, safe, and sanitary housing in the private market.
- **National Parks:** Construction and renovation projects would be prevented or delayed at two national parks in Idaho: Craters Of The Moon National Preserve and Minidoka National Historic Site.

Balances Only with Gimmicks and Deep Cuts to Programs that Serve the Most Vulnerable and Help Expand Opportunity. On top of their cuts to middle-class investments and the ACA, the Republican budgets would cut:

- **Pell Grants:** Republican reductions to Pell would reduce financial aid for the 54,000 Idaho students who rely on Pell grants to afford college.
- **Medicaid:** The House Republican proposal to block grant Medicaid would cut Federal funding to Idaho by approximately $3.8 billion over ten years, impacting children, seniors, and people with disabilities who rely on Medicaid.
- **Supplemental Nutrition Assistance Program (SNAP):** House Republican proposals to block grant and slash SNAP would cut nutrition aid in Idaho by an estimated $500 million over a five year period (2021-2025), jeopardizing nutrition assistance for the 212,000 Idaho residents who receive SNAP to help them put food on the table.

Fails to Address Our Crumbling Infrastructure: Republican budgets lack a real plan to address the looming expiration and insolvency of the Highway Trust Fund. Through the Highway Trust Fund, in FY 2014 the Federal Government obligated $286.2 million to Idaho through the Federal Aid Highways program for highway planning and construction and over $21.9 million through Transit Formula Grants that support our Nation's mass transit systems.

i. Numbers are rounded. For a description of how impacts were calculated, see http://go.wh.gov/RoNU1j

THE WHITE HOUSE

Office of the Press Secretary

FOR IMMEDIATE RELEASE

March 24, 2015

FACT SHEET: Republican Budget Resolutions: Same Failed Top-Down Economics for Illinois

With more than 12 million private-sector jobs created over the last 60 months, it is clear that the President's middle class economic agenda is working. But instead of taking the steps we need to strengthen the standing of working families, the Republican budgets for fiscal year (FY) 2016 would return our economy to the same top-down economics that has failed us before: cutting taxes for millionaires and billionaires, while slashing investments in the middle class that we need to grow the economy, like education, job training, and manufacturing. The Republican proposals stand in stark contrast to the President's FY 2016 Budget, which would bring middle class economics into the 21st Century. A state-by-state breakdown of this contrast, including how the Republican budgets affect Illinois, can be found in a report released today here: http://go.wh.gov/RoNU1j.

The President's Budget builds on the progress we've made and shows what we can do if we invest in America's future and commit to an economy that rewards hard work, generates rising incomes, and allows everyone to share in the prosperity of a growing America. It lays out a strategy to strengthen our middle class and help America's hard-working families get ahead in a time of relentless economic and technological change. And it makes the critical investments needed to accelerate and sustain economic growth in the long run, including in research, education, training, and infrastructure.

Republicans have chosen different priorities. Yet again, they are seeking to balance the budget on the backs of the middle class, while cutting taxes for the wealthy and well-connected. They still won't say where many of their spending cuts come from. But they are clear that their budgets would continue the harmful cuts known as sequestration in 2016, threatening economic growth, cutting programs middle-class families count on, and attempting to fund national security through irresponsible budget gimmicks. Their budgets slash domestic investments that support the middle-class even more significantly after 2016, along with programs that serve the most vulnerable Americans. House Republicans would end Medicare as we know it, transforming it from a guarantee seniors can count on into a voucher program. After five years of the Affordable Care Act, more than 16 million people have gained coverage. Yet once again, the Republican budgets propose to repeal the Affordable Care Act's coverage expansions.

The choice could not be more clear or the consequences more stark. Thanks to President Obama and the resilience of the American people, the economy is growing

again. The Republican budgets would put that growth at risk and limit opportunity for the middle-class and those seeking to join it.

In Illinois, the Republican budgets would[i]:

Cut Taxes for Millionaires and Raise Taxes for Working Families and Students:
While claiming to prioritize fiscal responsibility, the Republican budgets would not ask the wealthy to contribute a single dollar to deficit reduction, and the proposals specified in the House budget would cut taxes for millionaires by an average of at least $50,000. Meanwhile, the Republican budgets do nothing to prevent tax increases averaging $1,100 for 12 million families and students paying for college and $900 for 16 million working families with children. In 2015, 629,000 Illinois families will receive a total of $577 million in tax cuts from improvements to pro-work tax credits that would expire after 2017 under the Republican budgets.

Eliminate Affordable Health Care: The Affordable Care Act is working. After five years of the Affordable Care Act, more than 16 million people have gained coverage. Yet once again, the Republican budgets propose to repeal the Affordable Care Act's coverage expansions, taking away health insurance from millions of people. In particular, the Republican budgets would eliminate coverage for 349,000 Illinois residents who have newly signed up for coverage or re-enrolled through the Marketplaces. Some of these individuals would become uninsured while others would end up with worse or less affordable coverage.

Raise Health Care Costs for Seniors: 194,300 Illinois seniors and people with disabilities benefited by an average of $930 from the closure of the Medicare Part D prescription drug donut hole in 2014 alone. Under the Republican plan to repeal the Affordable Care Act, at least that many would likely have to pay more for needed medications in future years. The House budget would also end Medicare as we know it, replacing guaranteed access to the traditional Medicare program with a voucher program, risking a death spiral in traditional Medicare.

Slash Investments in the Middle Class: Under the Republican budgets, both non-defense and base defense discretionary funding in 2016 would be at the lowest real levels in a decade. Compared to the President's Budget, if the Republican budgets were to take effect, these are just some of the impacts on Illinois:

- **Head Start:** 1,480 fewer children in Illinois would have access to Head Start services, representing a permanently missed opportunity to help these children enter elementary school ready to succeed.
- **Teachers and Schools:** Illinois would receive $58.2 million less funding for disadvantaged students, an amount that is enough to fund about 210 schools, 800 teacher and aide jobs, and 69,000 students.

- **Education for Children with Disabilities:** Illinois would receive $14.2 million less funding to provide educational opportunities for students with disabilities, representing an approximately 2.8 percent cut and shifting the burden for meeting these children's needs to Illinois and its local communities.
- **Job Training and Employment Services:** 94,300 fewer Illinois residents would receive job training and employment services, including help finding jobs and skills training.
- **Affordable Housing:** Illinois would receive approximately $80.6 million less in Federal funding, resulting in 5,040 fewer families receiving Housing Choice Vouchers, which enable very low-income families to afford decent, safe, and sanitary housing in the private market.

Balances Only with Gimmicks and Deep Cuts to Programs that Serve the Most Vulnerable and Help Expand Opportunity. On top of their cuts to middle-class investments and the ACA, the Republican budgets would cut:

- **Pell Grants:** Republican reductions to Pell would reduce financial aid for the 352,000 Illinois students who rely on Pell grants to afford college.
- **Medicaid:** The House Republican proposal to block grant Medicaid would cut Federal funding to Illinois by approximately $29.8 billion over ten years, impacting children, seniors, and people with disabilities who rely on Medicaid.
- **Supplemental Nutrition Assistance Program (SNAP):** House Republican proposals to block grant and slash SNAP would cut nutrition aid in Illinois by an estimated $5.1 billion over a five year period (2021-2025), jeopardizing nutrition assistance for the 2,015,000 Illinois residents who receive SNAP to help them put food on the table.

Fails to Address Our Crumbling Infrastructure: Republican budgets lack a real plan to address the looming expiration and insolvency of the Highway Trust Fund. Through the Highway Trust Fund, in FY 2014 the Federal Government obligated $1.4 billion to Illinois through the Federal Aid Highways program for highway planning and construction and over $848.1 million through Transit Formula Grants that support our Nation's mass transit systems.

i. Numbers are rounded. For a description of how impacts were calculated, see http://go.wh.gov/RoNU1j

THE WHITE HOUSE
Office of the Press Secretary

FOR IMMEDIATE RELEASE
March 24, 2015

FACT SHEET: Republican Budget Resolutions: Same Failed Top-Down Economics for Indiana

With more than 12 million private-sector jobs created over the last 60 months, it is clear that the President's middle class economic agenda is working. But instead of taking the steps we need to strengthen the standing of working families, the Republican budgets for fiscal year (FY) 2016 would return our economy to the same top-down economics that has failed us before: cutting taxes for millionaires and billionaires, while slashing investments in the middle class that we need to grow the economy, like education, job training, and manufacturing. The Republican proposals stand in stark contrast to the President's FY 2016 Budget, which would bring middle class economics into the 21st Century. A state-by-state breakdown of this contrast, including how the Republican budgets affect Indiana, can be found in a report released today here: http://go.wh.gov/RoNU1j.

The President's Budget builds on the progress we've made and shows what we can do if we invest in America's future and commit to an economy that rewards hard work, generates rising incomes, and allows everyone to share in the prosperity of a growing America. It lays out a strategy to strengthen our middle class and help America's hard-working families get ahead in a time of relentless economic and technological change. And it makes the critical investments needed to accelerate and sustain economic growth in the long run, including in research, education, training, and infrastructure.

Republicans have chosen different priorities. Yet again, they are seeking to balance the budget on the backs of the middle class, while cutting taxes for the wealthy and well-connected. They still won't say where many of their spending cuts come from. But they are clear that their budgets would continue the harmful cuts known as sequestration in 2016, threatening economic growth, cutting programs middle-class families count on, and attempting to fund national security through irresponsible budget gimmicks. Their budgets slash domestic investments that support the middle-class even more significantly after 2016, along with programs that serve the most vulnerable Americans. House Republicans would end Medicare as we know it, transforming it from a guarantee seniors can count on into a voucher program. After five years of the Affordable Care Act, more than 16 million people have gained coverage. Yet once again, the Republican budgets propose to repeal the Affordable Care Act's coverage expansions.

The choice could not be more clear or the consequences more stark. Thanks to President Obama and the resilience of the American people, the economy is growing

again. The Republican budgets would put that growth at risk and limit opportunity for the middle-class and those seeking to join it.

In Indiana, the Republican budgets would[i]:

Cut Taxes for Millionaires and Raise Taxes for Working Families and Students: While claiming to prioritize fiscal responsibility, the Republican budgets would not ask the wealthy to contribute a single dollar to deficit reduction, and the proposals specified in the House budget would cut taxes for millionaires by an average of at least $50,000. Meanwhile, the Republican budgets do nothing to prevent tax increases averaging $1,100 for 12 million families and students paying for college and $900 for 16 million working families with children. In 2015, 327,000 Indiana families will receive a total of $300 million in tax cuts from improvements to pro-work tax credits that would expire after 2017 under the Republican budgets.

Eliminate Affordable Health Care: The Affordable Care Act is working. After five years of the Affordable Care Act, more than 16 million people have gained coverage. Yet once again, the Republican budgets propose to repeal the Affordable Care Act's coverage expansions, taking away health insurance from millions of people. In particular, the Republican budgets would eliminate coverage for 219,000 Indiana residents who have newly signed up for coverage or re-enrolled through the Marketplaces. Some of these individuals would become uninsured while others would end up with worse or less affordable coverage.

Raise Health Care Costs for Seniors: 126,500 Indiana seniors and people with disabilities benefited by an average of $930 from the closure of the Medicare Part D prescription drug donut hole in 2014 alone. Under the Republican plan to repeal the Affordable Care Act, at least that many would likely have to pay more for needed medications in future years. The House budget would also end Medicare as we know it, replacing guaranteed access to the traditional Medicare program with a voucher program, risking a death spiral in traditional Medicare.

Slash Investments in the Middle Class: Under the Republican budgets, both non-defense and base defense discretionary funding in 2016 would be at the lowest real levels in a decade. Compared to the President's Budget, if the Republican budgets were to take effect, these are just some of the impacts on Indiana:

- **Head Start:** 520 fewer children in Indiana would have access to Head Start services, representing a permanently missed opportunity to help these children enter elementary school ready to succeed.
- **Teachers and Schools:** Indiana would receive $20.4 million less funding for disadvantaged students, an amount that is enough to fund about 70 schools, 280 teacher and aide jobs, and 22,000 students.

- **Education for Children with Disabilities:** Indiana would receive $7.2 million less funding to provide educational opportunities for students with disabilities, representing an approximately 2.8 percent cut and shifting the burden for meeting these children's needs to Indiana and its local communities.
- **Job Training and Employment Services:** 43,400 fewer Indiana residents would receive job training and employment services, including help finding jobs and skills training.
- **Affordable Housing**: Indiana would receive approximately $19.5 million less in Federal funding, resulting in 2,130 fewer families receiving Housing Choice Vouchers, which enable very low-income families to afford decent, safe, and sanitary housing in the private market.

Balances Only with Gimmicks and Deep Cuts to Programs that Serve the Most Vulnerable and Help Expand Opportunity. On top of their cuts to middle-class investments and the ACA, the Republican budgets would cut:

- **Pell Grants:** Republican reductions to Pell would reduce financial aid for the 182,000 Indiana students who rely on Pell grants to afford college.
- **Medicaid:** The House Republican proposal to block grant Medicaid would cut Federal funding to Indiana by approximately $20.0 billion over ten years, impacting children, seniors, and people with disabilities who rely on Medicaid.
- **Supplemental Nutrition Assistance Program (SNAP):** House Republican proposals to block grant and slash SNAP would cut nutrition aid in Indiana by an estimated $2.1 billion over a five year period (2021-2025), jeopardizing nutrition assistance for the 893,000 Indiana residents who receive SNAP to help them put food on the table.

Fails to Address Our Crumbling Infrastructure: Republican budgets lack a real plan to address the looming expiration and insolvency of the Highway Trust Fund. Through the Highway Trust Fund, in FY 2014 the Federal Government obligated $981.6 million to Indiana through the Federal Aid Highways program for highway planning and construction and over $134.7 million through Transit Formula Grants that support our Nation's mass transit systems.

i. Numbers are rounded. For a description of how impacts were calculated, see http://go.wh.gov/RoNU1j

THE WHITE HOUSE
Office of the Press Secretary

FOR IMMEDIATE RELEASE
March 24, 2015

FACT SHEET: Republican Budget Resolutions: Same Failed Top-Down Economics for Iowa

With more than 12 million private-sector jobs created over the last 60 months, it is clear that the President's middle class economic agenda is working. But instead of taking the steps we need to strengthen the standing of working families, the Republican budgets for fiscal year (FY) 2016 would return our economy to the same top-down economics that has failed us before: cutting taxes for millionaires and billionaires, while slashing investments in the middle class that we need to grow the economy, like education, job training, and manufacturing. The Republican proposals stand in stark contrast to the President's FY 2016 Budget, which would bring middle class economics into the 21st Century. A state-by-state breakdown of this contrast, including how the Republican budgets affect Iowa, can be found in a report released today here: http://go.wh.gov/RoNU1j.

The President's Budget builds on the progress we've made and shows what we can do if we invest in America's future and commit to an economy that rewards hard work, generates rising incomes, and allows everyone to share in the prosperity of a growing America. It lays out a strategy to strengthen our middle class and help America's hard-working families get ahead in a time of relentless economic and technological change. And it makes the critical investments needed to accelerate and sustain economic growth in the long run, including in research, education, training, and infrastructure.

Republicans have chosen different priorities. Yet again, they are seeking to balance the budget on the backs of the middle class, while cutting taxes for the wealthy and well-connected. They still won't say where many of their spending cuts come from. But they are clear that their budgets would continue the harmful cuts known as sequestration in 2016, threatening economic growth, cutting programs middle-class families count on, and attempting to fund national security through irresponsible budget gimmicks. Their budgets slash domestic investments that support the middle-class even more significantly after 2016, along with programs that serve the most vulnerable Americans. House Republicans would end Medicare as we know it, transforming it from a guarantee seniors can count on into a voucher program. After five years of the Affordable Care Act, more than 16 million people have gained coverage. Yet once again, the Republican budgets propose to repeal the Affordable Care Act's coverage expansions.

The choice could not be more clear or the consequences more stark. Thanks to President Obama and the resilience of the American people, the economy is growing

again. The Republican budgets would put that growth at risk and limit opportunity for the middle-class and those seeking to join it.

In Iowa, the Republican budgets would[i]:

Cut Taxes for Millionaires and Raise Taxes for Working Families and Students: While claiming to prioritize fiscal responsibility, the Republican budgets would not ask the wealthy to contribute a single dollar to deficit reduction, and the proposals specified in the House budget would cut taxes for millionaires by an average of at least $50,000. Meanwhile, the Republican budgets do nothing to prevent tax increases averaging $1,100 for 12 million families and students paying for college and $900 for 16 million working families with children. In 2015, 120,000 Iowa families will receive a total of $105 million in tax cuts from improvements to pro-work tax credits that would expire after 2017 under the Republican budgets.

Eliminate Affordable Health Care: The Affordable Care Act is working. After five years of the Affordable Care Act, more than 16 million people have gained coverage. Yet once again, the Republican budgets propose to repeal the Affordable Care Act's coverage expansions, taking away health insurance from millions of people. In particular, the Republican budgets would eliminate coverage for 45,000 Iowa residents who have newly signed up for coverage or re-enrolled through the Marketplaces. Some of these individuals would become uninsured while others would end up with worse or less affordable coverage.

Raise Health Care Costs for Seniors: 54,300 Iowa seniors and people with disabilities benefited by an average of $850 from the closure of the Medicare Part D prescription drug donut hole in 2014 alone. Under the Republican plan to repeal the Affordable Care Act, at least that many would likely have to pay more for needed medications in future years. The House budget would also end Medicare as we know it, replacing guaranteed access to the traditional Medicare program with a voucher program, risking a death spiral in traditional Medicare.

Slash Investments in the Middle Class: Under the Republican budgets, both non-defense and base defense discretionary funding in 2016 would be at the lowest real levels in a decade. Compared to the President's Budget, if the Republican budgets were to take effect, these are just some of the impacts on Iowa:

- **Head Start:** 280 fewer children in Iowa would have access to Head Start services, representing a permanently missed opportunity to help these children enter elementary school ready to succeed.
- **Teachers and Schools:** Iowa would receive $7.6 million less funding for disadvantaged students, an amount that is enough to fund about 50 schools, 100 teacher and aide jobs, and 8,000 students.

- **Education for Children with Disabilities:** Iowa would receive $3.4 million less funding to provide educational opportunities for students with disabilities, representing an approximately 2.8 percent cut and shifting the burden for meeting these children's needs to Iowa and its local communities.
- **Job Training and Employment Services:** 20,500 fewer Iowa residents would receive job training and employment services, including help finding jobs and skills training.
- **Affordable Housing**: Iowa would receive approximately $9.1 million less in Federal funding, resulting in 1,230 fewer families receiving Housing Choice Vouchers, which enable very low-income families to afford decent, safe, and sanitary housing in the private market.
- **National Parks:** Construction and renovation projects would be prevented or delayed at Herbert Hoover National Historic Site.

Balances Only with Gimmicks and Deep Cuts to Programs that Serve the Most Vulnerable and Help Expand Opportunity. On top of their cuts to middle-class investments and the ACA, the Republican budgets would cut:

- **Pell Grants:** Republican reductions to Pell would reduce financial aid for the 112,000 Iowa students who rely on Pell grants to afford college.
- **Medicaid:** The House Republican proposal to block grant Medicaid would cut Federal funding to Iowa by approximately $8.0 billion over ten years, impacting children, seniors, and people with disabilities who rely on Medicaid.
- **Supplemental Nutrition Assistance Program (SNAP):** House Republican proposals to block grant and slash SNAP would cut nutrition aid in Iowa by an estimated $800 million over a five year period (2021-2025), jeopardizing nutrition assistance for the 408,000 Iowa residents who receive SNAP to help them put food on the table.

Fails to Address Our Crumbling Infrastructure: Republican budgets lack a real plan to address the looming expiration and insolvency of the Highway Trust Fund. Through the Highway Trust Fund, in FY 2014 the Federal Government obligated $505.3 million to Iowa through the Federal Aid Highways program for highway planning and construction and over $63.6 million through Transit Formula Grants that support our Nation's mass transit systems.

i. Numbers are rounded. For a description of how impacts were calculated, see http://go.wh.gov/RoNU1j

THE WHITE HOUSE
Office of the Press Secretary

FOR IMMEDIATE RELEASE
March 24, 2015

FACT SHEET: Republican Budget Resolutions: Same Failed Top-Down Economics for Kansas

With more than 12 million private-sector jobs created over the last 60 months, it is clear that the President's middle class economic agenda is working. But instead of taking the steps we need to strengthen the standing of working families, the Republican budgets for fiscal year (FY) 2016 would return our economy to the same top-down economics that has failed us before: cutting taxes for millionaires and billionaires, while slashing investments in the middle class that we need to grow the economy, like education, job training, and manufacturing. The Republican proposals stand in stark contrast to the President's FY 2016 Budget, which would bring middle class economics into the 21st Century. A state-by-state breakdown of this contrast, including how the Republican budgets affect Kansas, can be found in a report released today here: http://go.wh.gov/RoNU1j.

The President's Budget builds on the progress we've made and shows what we can do if we invest in America's future and commit to an economy that rewards hard work, generates rising incomes, and allows everyone to share in the prosperity of a growing America. It lays out a strategy to strengthen our middle class and help America's hard-working families get ahead in a time of relentless economic and technological change. And it makes the critical investments needed to accelerate and sustain economic growth in the long run, including in research, education, training, and infrastructure.

Republicans have chosen different priorities. Yet again, they are seeking to balance the budget on the backs of the middle class, while cutting taxes for the wealthy and well-connected. They still won't say where many of their spending cuts come from. But they are clear that their budgets would continue the harmful cuts known as sequestration in 2016, threatening economic growth, cutting programs middle-class families count on, and attempting to fund national security through irresponsible budget gimmicks. Their budgets slash domestic investments that support the middle-class even more significantly after 2016, along with programs that serve the most vulnerable Americans. House Republicans would end Medicare as we know it, transforming it from a guarantee seniors can count on into a voucher program. After five years of the Affordable Care Act, more than 16 million people have gained coverage. Yet once again, the Republican budgets propose to repeal the Affordable Care Act's coverage expansions.

The choice could not be more clear or the consequences more stark. Thanks to President Obama and the resilience of the American people, the economy is growing

again. The Republican budgets would put that growth at risk and limit opportunity for the middle-class and those seeking to join it.

In Kansas, the Republican budgets would[i]:

Cut Taxes for Millionaires and Raise Taxes for Working Families and Students: While claiming to prioritize fiscal responsibility, the Republican budgets would not ask the wealthy to contribute a single dollar to deficit reduction, and the proposals specified in the House budget would cut taxes for millionaires by an average of at least $50,000. Meanwhile, the Republican budgets do nothing to prevent tax increases averaging $1,100 for 12 million families and students paying for college and $900 for 16 million working families with children. In 2015, 134,000 Kansas families will receive a total of $121 million in tax cuts from improvements to pro-work tax credits that would expire after 2017 under the Republican budgets.

Eliminate Affordable Health Care: The Affordable Care Act is working. After five years of the Affordable Care Act, more than 16 million people have gained coverage. Yet once again, the Republican budgets propose to repeal the Affordable Care Act's coverage expansions, taking away health insurance from millions of people. In particular, the Republican budgets would eliminate coverage for 96,000 Kansas residents who have newly signed up for coverage or re-enrolled through the Marketplaces. Some of these individuals would become uninsured while others would end up with worse or less affordable coverage.

Raise Health Care Costs for Seniors: 46,800 Kansas seniors and people with disabilities benefited by an average of $830 from the closure of the Medicare Part D prescription drug donut hole in 2014 alone. Under the Republican plan to repeal the Affordable Care Act, at least that many would likely have to pay more for needed medications in future years. The House budget would also end Medicare as we know it, replacing guaranteed access to the traditional Medicare program with a voucher program, risking a death spiral in traditional Medicare.

Slash Investments in the Middle Class: Under the Republican budgets, both non-defense and base defense discretionary funding in 2016 would be at the lowest real levels in a decade. Compared to the President's Budget, if the Republican budgets were to take effect, these are just some of the impacts on Kansas:

- **Head Start:** 280 fewer children in Kansas would have access to Head Start services, representing a permanently missed opportunity to help these children enter elementary school ready to succeed.
- **Teachers and Schools:** Kansas would receive $8.6 million less funding for disadvantaged students, an amount that is enough to fund about 50 schools, 120 teacher and aide jobs, and 12,000 students.

- **Education for Children with Disabilities:** Kansas would receive $3.0 million less funding to provide educational opportunities for students with disabilities, representing an approximately 2.8 percent cut and shifting the burden for meeting these children's needs to Kansas and its local communities.
- **Job Training and Employment Services:** 18,700 fewer Kansas residents would receive job training and employment services, including help finding jobs and skills training.
- **Affordable Housing**: Kansas would receive approximately $5.8 million less in Federal funding, resulting in 710 fewer families receiving Housing Choice Vouchers, which enable very low-income families to afford decent, safe, and sanitary housing in the private market.
- **National Parks:** Construction and renovation projects would be prevented or delayed at Fort Larned National Historic Site.

Balances Only with Gimmicks and Deep Cuts to Programs that Serve the Most Vulnerable and Help Expand Opportunity. On top of their cuts to middle-class investments and the ACA, the Republican budgets would cut:

- **Pell Grants:** Republican reductions to Pell would reduce financial aid for the 72,000 Kansas students who rely on Pell grants to afford college.
- **Medicaid:** The House Republican proposal to block grant Medicaid would cut Federal funding to Kansas by approximately $5.3 billion over ten years, impacting children, seniors, and people with disabilities who rely on Medicaid.
- **Supplemental Nutrition Assistance Program (SNAP):** House Republican proposals to block grant and slash SNAP would cut nutrition aid in Kansas by an estimated $600 million over a five year period (2021-2025), jeopardizing nutrition assistance for the 293,000 Kansas residents who receive SNAP to help them put food on the table.

Fails to Address Our Crumbling Infrastructure: Republican budgets lack a real plan to address the looming expiration and insolvency of the Highway Trust Fund. Through the Highway Trust Fund, in FY 2014 the Federal Government obligated $364.2 million to Kansas through the Federal Aid Highways program for highway planning and construction and over $44.9 million through Transit Formula Grants that support our Nation's mass transit systems.

i. Numbers are rounded. For a description of how impacts were calculated, see http://go.wh.gov/RoNU1j

FOR IMMEDIATE RELEASE
March 24, 2015

FACT SHEET: Republican Budget Resolutions: Same Failed Top-Down Economics for Kentucky

With more than 12 million private-sector jobs created over the last 60 months, it is clear that the President's middle class economic agenda is working. But instead of taking the steps we need to strengthen the standing of working families, the Republican budgets for fiscal year (FY) 2016 would return our economy to the same top-down economics that has failed us before: cutting taxes for millionaires and billionaires, while slashing investments in the middle class that we need to grow the economy, like education, job training, and manufacturing. The Republican proposals stand in stark contrast to the President's FY 2016 Budget, which would bring middle class economics into the 21st Century. A state-by-state breakdown of this contrast, including how the Republican budgets affect Kentucky, can be found in a report released today here: http://go.wh.gov/RoNU1j.

The President's Budget builds on the progress we've made and shows what we can do if we invest in America's future and commit to an economy that rewards hard work, generates rising incomes, and allows everyone to share in the prosperity of a growing America. It lays out a strategy to strengthen our middle class and help America's hard-working families get ahead in a time of relentless economic and technological change. And it makes the critical investments needed to accelerate and sustain economic growth in the long run, including in research, education, training, and infrastructure.

Republicans have chosen different priorities. Yet again, they are seeking to balance the budget on the backs of the middle class, while cutting taxes for the wealthy and well-connected. They still won't say where many of their spending cuts come from. But they are clear that their budgets would continue the harmful cuts known as sequestration in 2016, threatening economic growth, cutting programs middle-class families count on, and attempting to fund national security through irresponsible budget gimmicks. Their budgets slash domestic investments that support the middle-class even more significantly after 2016, along with programs that serve the most vulnerable Americans. House Republicans would end Medicare as we know it, transforming it from a guarantee seniors can count on into a voucher program. After five years of the Affordable Care Act, more than 16 million people have gained coverage. Yet once again, the Republican budgets propose to repeal the Affordable Care Act's coverage expansions.

The choice could not be more clear or the consequences more stark. Thanks to President Obama and the resilience of the American people, the economy is growing

again. The Republican budgets would put that growth at risk and limit opportunity for the middle-class and those seeking to join it.

In Kentucky, the Republican budgets would[i]:

Cut Taxes for Millionaires and Raise Taxes for Working Families and Students: While claiming to prioritize fiscal responsibility, the Republican budgets would not ask the wealthy to contribute a single dollar to deficit reduction, and the proposals specified in the House budget would cut taxes for millionaires by an average of at least $50,000. Meanwhile, the Republican budgets do nothing to prevent tax increases averaging $1,100 for 12 million families and students paying for college and $900 for 16 million working families with children. In 2015, 234,000 Kentucky families will receive a total of $205 million in tax cuts from improvements to pro-work tax credits that would expire after 2017 under the Republican budgets.

Eliminate Affordable Health Care: The Affordable Care Act is working. After five years of the Affordable Care Act, more than 16 million people have gained coverage. Yet once again, the Republican budgets propose to repeal the Affordable Care Act's coverage expansions, taking away health insurance from millions of people. In particular, the Republican budgets would eliminate coverage for 106,000 Kentucky residents who have newly signed up for coverage or re-enrolled through the Marketplaces. Some of these individuals would become uninsured while others would end up with worse or less affordable coverage.

Raise Health Care Costs for Seniors: 92,000 Kentucky seniors and people with disabilities benefited by an average of $980 from the closure of the Medicare Part D prescription drug donut hole in 2014 alone. Under the Republican plan to repeal the Affordable Care Act, at least that many would likely have to pay more for needed medications in future years. The House budget would also end Medicare as we know it, replacing guaranteed access to the traditional Medicare program with a voucher program, risking a death spiral in traditional Medicare.

Slash Investments in the Middle Class: Under the Republican budgets, both non-defense and base defense discretionary funding in 2016 would be at the lowest real levels in a decade. Compared to the President's Budget, if the Republican budgets were to take effect, these are just some of the impacts on Kentucky:

- **Head Start:** 590 fewer children in Kentucky would have access to Head Start services, representing a permanently missed opportunity to help these children enter elementary school ready to succeed.
- **Teachers and Schools:** Kentucky would receive $16.9 million less funding for disadvantaged students, an amount that is enough to fund about 70 schools, 230 teacher and aide jobs, and 36,000 students.

- **Education for Children with Disabilities:** Kentucky would receive $4.4 million less funding to provide educational opportunities for students with disabilities, representing an approximately 2.8 percent cut and shifting the burden for meeting these children's needs to Kentucky and its local communities.
- **Job Training and Employment Services:** 28,800 fewer Kentucky residents would receive job training and employment services, including help finding jobs and skills training.
- **Affordable Housing**: Kentucky would receive approximately $18.5 million less in Federal funding, resulting in 1,830 fewer families receiving Housing Choice Vouchers, which enable very low-income families to afford decent, safe, and sanitary housing in the private market.

Balances Only with Gimmicks and Deep Cuts to Programs that Serve the Most Vulnerable and Help Expand Opportunity. On top of their cuts to middle-class investments and the ACA, the Republican budgets would cut:

- **Pell Grants:** Republican reductions to Pell would reduce financial aid for the 118,000 Kentucky students who rely on Pell grants to afford college.
- **Medicaid:** The House Republican proposal to block grant Medicaid would cut Federal funding to Kentucky by approximately $18.9 billion over ten years, impacting children, seniors, and people with disabilities who rely on Medicaid.
- **Supplemental Nutrition Assistance Program (SNAP):** House Republican proposals to block grant and slash SNAP would cut nutrition aid in Kentucky by an estimated $1.9 billion over a five year period (2021-2025), jeopardizing nutrition assistance for the 828,000 Kentucky residents who receive SNAP to help them put food on the table.

Fails to Address Our Crumbling Infrastructure: Republican budgets lack a real plan to address the looming expiration and insolvency of the Highway Trust Fund. Through the Highway Trust Fund, in FY 2014 the Federal Government obligated $686.0 million to Kentucky through the Federal Aid Highways program for highway planning and construction and over $100.6 million through Transit Formula Grants that support our Nation's mass transit systems.

i. Numbers are rounded. For a description of how impacts were calculated, see http://go.wh.gov/RoNU1j

THE WHITE HOUSE
Office of the Press Secretary

FOR IMMEDIATE RELEASE
March 24, 2015

FACT SHEET: Republican Budget Resolutions: Same Failed Top-Down Economics for Louisiana

With more than 12 million private-sector jobs created over the last 60 months, it is clear that the President's middle class economic agenda is working. But instead of taking the steps we need to strengthen the standing of working families, the Republican budgets for fiscal year (FY) 2016 would return our economy to the same top-down economics that has failed us before: cutting taxes for millionaires and billionaires, while slashing investments in the middle class that we need to grow the economy, like education, job training, and manufacturing. The Republican proposals stand in stark contrast to the President's FY 2016 Budget, which would bring middle class economics into the 21st Century. A state-by-state breakdown of this contrast, including how the Republican budgets affect Louisiana, can be found in a report released today here: http://go.wh.gov/RoNU1j.

The President's Budget builds on the progress we've made and shows what we can do if we invest in America's future and commit to an economy that rewards hard work, generates rising incomes, and allows everyone to share in the prosperity of a growing America. It lays out a strategy to strengthen our middle class and help America's hard-working families get ahead in a time of relentless economic and technological change. And it makes the critical investments needed to accelerate and sustain economic growth in the long run, including in research, education, training, and infrastructure.

Republicans have chosen different priorities. Yet again, they are seeking to balance the budget on the backs of the middle class, while cutting taxes for the wealthy and well-connected. They still won't say where many of their spending cuts come from. But they are clear that their budgets would continue the harmful cuts known as sequestration in 2016, threatening economic growth, cutting programs middle-class families count on, and attempting to fund national security through irresponsible budget gimmicks. Their budgets slash domestic investments that support the middle-class even more significantly after 2016, along with programs that serve the most vulnerable Americans. House Republicans would end Medicare as we know it, transforming it from a guarantee seniors can count on into a voucher program. After five years of the Affordable Care Act, more than 16 million people have gained coverage. Yet once again, the Republican budgets propose to repeal the Affordable Care Act's coverage expansions.

The choice could not be more clear or the consequences more stark. Thanks to President Obama and the resilience of the American people, the economy is growing

again. The Republican budgets would put that growth at risk and limit opportunity for the middle-class and those seeking to join it.

In Louisiana, the Republican budgets would[i]:

Cut Taxes for Millionaires and Raise Taxes for Working Families and Students:
While claiming to prioritize fiscal responsibility, the Republican budgets would not ask the wealthy to contribute a single dollar to deficit reduction, and the proposals specified in the House budget would cut taxes for millionaires by an average of at least $50,000. Meanwhile, the Republican budgets do nothing to prevent tax increases averaging $1,100 for 12 million families and students paying for college and $900 for 16 million working families with children. In 2015, 279,000 Louisiana families will receive a total of $257 million in tax cuts from improvements to pro-work tax credits that would expire after 2017 under the Republican budgets.

Eliminate Affordable Health Care: The Affordable Care Act is working. After five years of the Affordable Care Act, more than 16 million people have gained coverage. Yet once again, the Republican budgets propose to repeal the Affordable Care Act's coverage expansions, taking away health insurance from millions of people. In particular, the Republican budgets would eliminate coverage for 186,000 Louisiana residents who have newly signed up for coverage or re-enrolled through the Marketplaces. Some of these individuals would become uninsured while others would end up with worse or less affordable coverage.

Raise Health Care Costs for Seniors: 73,300 Louisiana seniors and people with disabilities benefited by an average of $850 from the closure of the Medicare Part D prescription drug donut hole in 2014 alone. Under the Republican plan to repeal the Affordable Care Act, at least that many would likely have to pay more for needed medications in future years. The House budget would also end Medicare as we know it, replacing guaranteed access to the traditional Medicare program with a voucher program, risking a death spiral in traditional Medicare.

Slash Investments in the Middle Class: Under the Republican budgets, both non-defense and base defense discretionary funding in 2016 would be at the lowest real levels in a decade. Compared to the President's Budget, if the Republican budgets were to take effect, these are just some of the impacts on Louisiana:

- **Head Start:** 760 fewer children in Louisiana would have access to Head Start services, representing a permanently missed opportunity to help these children enter elementary school ready to succeed.
- **Teachers and Schools:** Louisiana would receive $23.4 million less funding for disadvantaged students, an amount that is enough to fund about 70 schools, 320 teacher and aide jobs, and 37,000 students.

- **Education for Children with Disabilities:** Louisiana would receive $5.5 million less funding to provide educational opportunities for students with disabilities, representing an approximately 2.9 percent cut and shifting the burden for meeting these children's needs to Louisiana and its local communities.
- **Job Training and Employment Services:** 27,500 fewer Louisiana residents would receive job training and employment services, including help finding jobs and skills training.
- **Affordable Housing:** Louisiana would receive approximately $32.5 million less in Federal funding, resulting in 2,900 fewer families receiving Housing Choice Vouchers, which enable very low-income families to afford decent, safe, and sanitary housing in the private market.
- **National Parks:** Construction and renovation projects would be prevented or delayed at Cane River Creole National Historical Park.

Balances Only with Gimmicks and Deep Cuts to Programs that Serve the Most Vulnerable and Help Expand Opportunity. On top of their cuts to middle-class investments and the ACA, the Republican budgets would cut:

- **Pell Grants:** Republican reductions to Pell would reduce financial aid for the 110,000 Louisiana students who rely on Pell grants to afford college.
- **Medicaid:** The House Republican proposal to block grant Medicaid would cut Federal funding to Louisiana by approximately $14.2 billion over ten years, impacting children, seniors, and people with disabilities who rely on Medicaid.
- **Supplemental Nutrition Assistance Program (SNAP):** House Republican proposals to block grant and slash SNAP would cut nutrition aid in Louisiana by an estimated $2 billion over a five year period (2021-2025), jeopardizing nutrition assistance for the 877,000 Louisiana residents who receive SNAP to help them put food on the table.

Fails to Address Our Crumbling Infrastructure: Republican budgets lack a real plan to address the looming expiration and insolvency of the Highway Trust Fund. Through the Highway Trust Fund, in FY 2014 the Federal Government obligated $749.9 million to Louisiana through the Federal Aid Highways program for highway planning and construction and over $50.7 million through Transit Formula Grants that support our Nation's mass transit systems.

i. Numbers are rounded. For a description of how impacts were calculated, see http://go.wh.gov/RoNU1j

FOR IMMEDIATE RELEASE
March 24, 2015

FACT SHEET: Republican Budget Resolutions: Same Failed Top-Down Economics for Maine

With more than 12 million private-sector jobs created over the last 60 months, it is clear that the President's middle class economic agenda is working. But instead of taking the steps we need to strengthen the standing of working families, the Republican budgets for fiscal year (FY) 2016 would return our economy to the same top-down economics that has failed us before: cutting taxes for millionaires and billionaires, while slashing investments in the middle class that we need to grow the economy, like education, job training, and manufacturing. The Republican proposals stand in stark contrast to the President's FY 2016 Budget, which would bring middle class economics into the 21st Century. A state-by-state breakdown of this contrast, including how the Republican budgets affect Maine, can be found in a report released today here: http://go.wh.gov/RoNU1j.

The President's Budget builds on the progress we've made and shows what we can do if we invest in America's future and commit to an economy that rewards hard work, generates rising incomes, and allows everyone to share in the prosperity of a growing America. It lays out a strategy to strengthen our middle class and help America's hard-working families get ahead in a time of relentless economic and technological change. And it makes the critical investments needed to accelerate and sustain economic growth in the long run, including in research, education, training, and infrastructure.

Republicans have chosen different priorities. Yet again, they are seeking to balance the budget on the backs of the middle class, while cutting taxes for the wealthy and well-connected. They still won't say where many of their spending cuts come from. But they are clear that their budgets would continue the harmful cuts known as sequestration in 2016, threatening economic growth, cutting programs middle-class families count on, and attempting to fund national security through irresponsible budget gimmicks. Their budgets slash domestic investments that support the middle-class even more significantly after 2016, along with programs that serve the most vulnerable Americans. House Republicans would end Medicare as we know it, transforming it from a guarantee seniors can count on into a voucher program. After five years of the Affordable Care Act, more than 16 million people have gained coverage. Yet once again, the Republican budgets propose to repeal the Affordable Care Act's coverage expansions.

The choice could not be more clear or the consequences more stark. Thanks to President Obama and the resilience of the American people, the economy is growing

again. The Republican budgets would put that growth at risk and limit opportunity for the middle-class and those seeking to join it.

In Maine, the Republican budgets would[i]:

Cut Taxes for Millionaires and Raise Taxes for Working Families and Students: While claiming to prioritize fiscal responsibility, the Republican budgets would not ask the wealthy to contribute a single dollar to deficit reduction, and the proposals specified in the House budget would cut taxes for millionaires by an average of at least $50,000. Meanwhile, the Republican budgets do nothing to prevent tax increases averaging $1,100 for 12 million families and students paying for college and $900 for 16 million working families with children. In 2015, 53,000 Maine families will receive a total of $43 million in tax cuts from improvements to pro-work tax credits that would expire after 2017 under the Republican budgets.

Eliminate Affordable Health Care: The Affordable Care Act is working. After five years of the Affordable Care Act, more than 16 million people have gained coverage. Yet once again, the Republican budgets propose to repeal the Affordable Care Act's coverage expansions, taking away health insurance from millions of people. In particular, the Republican budgets would eliminate coverage for 75,000 Maine residents who have newly signed up for coverage or re-enrolled through the Marketplaces. Some of these individuals would become uninsured while others would end up with worse or less affordable coverage.

Raise Health Care Costs for Seniors: 17,300 Maine seniors and people with disabilities benefited by an average of $870 from the closure of the Medicare Part D prescription drug donut hole in 2014 alone. Under the Republican plan to repeal the Affordable Care Act, at least that many would likely have to pay more for needed medications in future years. The House budget would also end Medicare as we know it, replacing guaranteed access to the traditional Medicare program with a voucher program, risking a death spiral in traditional Medicare.

Slash Investments in the Middle Class: Under the Republican budgets, both non-defense and base defense discretionary funding in 2016 would be at the lowest real levels in a decade. Compared to the President's Budget, if the Republican budgets were to take effect, these are just some of the impacts on Maine:

- **Head Start:** 150 fewer children in Maine would have access to Head Start services, representing a permanently missed opportunity to help these children enter elementary school ready to succeed.
- **Teachers and Schools:** Maine would receive $4.2 million less funding for disadvantaged students, an amount that is enough to fund about 30 schools, 60 teacher and aide jobs, and 3,000 students.

- **Education for Children with Disabilities:** Maine would receive $1.5 million less funding to provide educational opportunities for students with disabilities, representing an approximately 2.8 percent cut and shifting the burden for meeting these children's needs to Maine and its local communities.
- **Job Training and Employment Services:** 12,100 fewer Maine residents would receive job training and employment services, including help finding jobs and skills training.
- **Affordable Housing:** Maine would receive approximately $8.2 million less in Federal funding, resulting in 740 fewer families receiving Housing Choice Vouchers, which enable very low-income families to afford decent, safe, and sanitary housing in the private market.
- **National Parks:** Construction and renovation projects would be prevented or delayed at two national parks in Maine: Acadia National Park and Appalachian National Scenic Trail.

Balances Only with Gimmicks and Deep Cuts to Programs that Serve the Most Vulnerable and Help Expand Opportunity. On top of their cuts to middle-class investments and the ACA, the Republican budgets would cut:

- **Pell Grants:** Republican reductions to Pell would reduce financial aid for the 27,000 Maine students who rely on Pell grants to afford college.
- **Medicaid:** The House Republican proposal to block grant Medicaid would cut Federal funding to Maine by approximately $4.9 billion over ten years, impacting children, seniors, and people with disabilities who rely on Medicaid.
- **Supplemental Nutrition Assistance Program (SNAP):** House Republican proposals to block grant and slash SNAP would cut nutrition aid in Maine by an estimated $500 million over a five year period (2021-2025), jeopardizing nutrition assistance for the 231,000 Maine residents who receive SNAP to help them put food on the table.

Fails to Address Our Crumbling Infrastructure: Republican budgets lack a real plan to address the looming expiration and insolvency of the Highway Trust Fund. Through the Highway Trust Fund, in FY 2014 the Federal Government obligated $181.6 million to Maine through the Federal Aid Highways program for highway planning and construction and over $21.4 million through Transit Formula Grants that support our Nation's mass transit systems.

i. Numbers are rounded. For a description of how impacts were calculated, see http://go.wh.gov/RoNU1j

FOR IMMEDIATE RELEASE
March 24, 2015

FACT SHEET: Republican Budget Resolutions: Same Failed Top-Down Economics for Maryland

With more than 12 million private-sector jobs created over the last 60 months, it is clear that the President's middle class economic agenda is working. But instead of taking the steps we need to strengthen the standing of working families, the Republican budgets for fiscal year (FY) 2016 would return our economy to the same top-down economics that has failed us before: cutting taxes for millionaires and billionaires, while slashing investments in the middle class that we need to grow the economy, like education, job training, and manufacturing. The Republican proposals stand in stark contrast to the President's FY 2016 Budget, which would bring middle class economics into the 21st Century. A state-by-state breakdown of this contrast, including how the Republican budgets affect Maryland, can be found in a report released today here: http://go.wh.gov/RoNU1j.

The President's Budget builds on the progress we've made and shows what we can do if we invest in America's future and commit to an economy that rewards hard work, generates rising incomes, and allows everyone to share in the prosperity of a growing America. It lays out a strategy to strengthen our middle class and help America's hard-working families get ahead in a time of relentless economic and technological change. And it makes the critical investments needed to accelerate and sustain economic growth in the long run, including in research, education, training, and infrastructure.

Republicans have chosen different priorities. Yet again, they are seeking to balance the budget on the backs of the middle class, while cutting taxes for the wealthy and well-connected. They still won't say where many of their spending cuts come from. But they are clear that their budgets would continue the harmful cuts known as sequestration in 2016, threatening economic growth, cutting programs middle-class families count on, and attempting to fund national security through irresponsible budget gimmicks. Their budgets slash domestic investments that support the middle-class even more significantly after 2016, along with programs that serve the most vulnerable Americans. House Republicans would end Medicare as we know it, transforming it from a guarantee seniors can count on into a voucher program. After five years of the Affordable Care Act, more than 16 million people have gained coverage. Yet once again, the Republican budgets propose to repeal the Affordable Care Act's coverage expansions.

The choice could not be more clear or the consequences more stark. Thanks to President Obama and the resilience of the American people, the economy is growing

again. The Republican budgets would put that growth at risk and limit opportunity for the middle-class and those seeking to join it.

In Maryland, the Republican budgets would[i]:

Cut Taxes for Millionaires and Raise Taxes for Working Families and Students: While claiming to prioritize fiscal responsibility, the Republican budgets would not ask the wealthy to contribute a single dollar to deficit reduction, and the proposals specified in the House budget would cut taxes for millionaires by an average of at least $50,000. Meanwhile, the Republican budgets do nothing to prevent tax increases averaging $1,100 for 12 million families and students paying for college and $900 for 16 million working families with children. In 2015, 212,000 Maryland families will receive a total of $192 million in tax cuts from improvements to pro-work tax credits that would expire after 2017 under the Republican budgets.

Eliminate Affordable Health Care: The Affordable Care Act is working. After five years of the Affordable Care Act, more than 16 million people have gained coverage. Yet once again, the Republican budgets propose to repeal the Affordable Care Act's coverage expansions, taking away health insurance from millions of people. In particular, the Republican budgets would eliminate coverage for 120,000 Maryland residents who have newly signed up for coverage or re-enrolled through the Marketplaces. Some of these individuals would become uninsured while others would end up with worse or less affordable coverage.

Raise Health Care Costs for Seniors: 79,900 Maryland seniors and people with disabilities benefited by an average of $1,030 from the closure of the Medicare Part D prescription drug donut hole in 2014 alone. Under the Republican plan to repeal the Affordable Care Act, at least that many would likely have to pay more for needed medications in future years. The House budget would also end Medicare as we know it, replacing guaranteed access to the traditional Medicare program with a voucher program, risking a death spiral in traditional Medicare.

Slash Investments in the Middle Class: Under the Republican budgets, both non-defense and base defense discretionary funding in 2016 would be at the lowest real levels in a decade. Compared to the President's Budget, if the Republican budgets were to take effect, these are just some of the impacts on Maryland:

- **Head Start:** 420 fewer children in Maryland would have access to Head Start services, representing a permanently missed opportunity to help these children enter elementary school ready to succeed.
- **Teachers and Schools:** Maryland would receive $18.4 million less funding for disadvantaged students, an amount that is enough to fund about 30 schools, 250 teacher and aide jobs, and 15,000 students.

- **Education for Children with Disabilities:** Maryland would receive $5.6 million less funding to provide educational opportunities for students with disabilities, representing an approximately 2.8 percent cut and shifting the burden for meeting these children's needs to Maryland and its local communities.
- **Job Training and Employment Services:** 40,600 fewer Maryland residents would receive job training and employment services, including help finding jobs and skills training.
- **Affordable Housing**: Maryland would receive approximately $50.7 million less in Federal funding, resulting in 2,720 fewer families receiving Housing Choice Vouchers, which enable very low-income families to afford decent, safe, and sanitary housing in the private market.
- **National Parks:** Construction and renovation projects would be prevented or delayed at four national parks in Maryland: Assateague Island National Seashore, Chesapeake and Ohio Canal National Historical Park, Fort McHenry National Monument and Historic Shrine, and Hampton National Historic Site.

Balances Only with Gimmicks and Deep Cuts to Programs that Serve the Most Vulnerable and Help Expand Opportunity. On top of their cuts to middle-class investments and the ACA, the Republican budgets would cut:

- **Pell Grants:** Republican reductions to Pell would reduce financial aid for the 109,000 Maryland students who rely on Pell grants to afford college.
- **Medicaid:** The House Republican proposal to block grant Medicaid would cut Federal funding to Maryland by approximately $17.1 billion over ten years, impacting children, seniors, and people with disabilities who rely on Medicaid.
- **Supplemental Nutrition Assistance Program (SNAP):** House Republican proposals to block grant and slash SNAP would cut nutrition aid in Maryland by an estimated $1.8 billion over a five year period (2021-2025), jeopardizing nutrition assistance for the 788,000 Maryland residents who receive SNAP to help them put food on the table.

Fails to Address Our Crumbling Infrastructure: Republican budgets lack a real plan to address the looming expiration and insolvency of the Highway Trust Fund. Through the Highway Trust Fund, in FY 2014 the Federal Government obligated $527.5 million to Maryland through the Federal Aid Highways program for highway planning and construction and over $376.5 million through Transit Formula Grants that support our Nation's mass transit systems.

###

i. Numbers are rounded. For a description of how impacts were calculated, see http://go.wh.gov/RoNU1j

FOR IMMEDIATE RELEASE
March 24, 2015

FACT SHEET: Republican Budget Resolutions: Same Failed Top-Down Economics for Massachusetts

With more than 12 million private-sector jobs created over the last 60 months, it is clear that the President's middle class economic agenda is working. But instead of taking the steps we need to strengthen the standing of working families, the Republican budgets for fiscal year (FY) 2016 would return our economy to the same top-down economics that has failed us before: cutting taxes for millionaires and billionaires, while slashing investments in the middle class that we need to grow the economy, like education, job training, and manufacturing. The Republican proposals stand in stark contrast to the President's FY 2016 Budget, which would bring middle class economics into the 21st Century. A state-by-state breakdown of this contrast, including how the Republican budgets affect Massachusetts, can be found in a report released today here: http://go.wh.gov/RoNU1j.

The President's Budget builds on the progress we've made and shows what we can do if we invest in America's future and commit to an economy that rewards hard work, generates rising incomes, and allows everyone to share in the prosperity of a growing America. It lays out a strategy to strengthen our middle class and help America's hard-working families get ahead in a time of relentless economic and technological change. And it makes the critical investments needed to accelerate and sustain economic growth in the long run, including in research, education, training, and infrastructure.

Republicans have chosen different priorities. Yet again, they are seeking to balance the budget on the backs of the middle class, while cutting taxes for the wealthy and well-connected. They still won't say where many of their spending cuts come from. But they are clear that their budgets would continue the harmful cuts known as sequestration in 2016, threatening economic growth, cutting programs middle-class families count on, and attempting to fund national security through irresponsible budget gimmicks. Their budgets slash domestic investments that support the middle-class even more significantly after 2016, along with programs that serve the most vulnerable Americans. House Republicans would end Medicare as we know it, transforming it from a guarantee seniors can count on into a voucher program. After five years of the Affordable Care Act, more than 16 million people have gained coverage. Yet once again, the Republican budgets propose to repeal the Affordable Care Act's coverage expansions.

The choice could not be more clear or the consequences more stark. Thanks to President Obama and the resilience of the American people, the economy is growing

again. The Republican budgets would put that growth at risk and limit opportunity for the middle-class and those seeking to join it.

In Massachusetts, the Republican budgets would[i]:

Cut Taxes for Millionaires and Raise Taxes for Working Families and Students: While claiming to prioritize fiscal responsibility, the Republican budgets would not ask the wealthy to contribute a single dollar to deficit reduction, and the proposals specified in the House budget would cut taxes for millionaires by an average of at least $50,000. Meanwhile, the Republican budgets do nothing to prevent tax increases averaging $1,100 for 12 million families and students paying for college and $900 for 16 million working families with children. In 2015, 195,000 Massachusetts families will receive a total of $166 million in tax cuts from improvements to pro-work tax credits that would expire after 2017 under the Republican budgets.

Eliminate Affordable Health Care: The Affordable Care Act is working. After five years of the Affordable Care Act, more than 16 million people have gained coverage. Yet once again, the Republican budgets propose to repeal the Affordable Care Act's coverage expansions, taking away health insurance from millions of people. In particular, the Republican budgets would eliminate coverage for 141,000 Massachusetts residents who have newly signed up for coverage or re-enrolled through the Marketplaces. Some of these individuals would become uninsured while others would end up with worse or less affordable coverage.

Raise Health Care Costs for Seniors: 79,800 Massachusetts seniors and people with disabilities benefited by an average of $920 from the closure of the Medicare Part D prescription drug donut hole in 2014 alone. Under the Republican plan to repeal the Affordable Care Act, at least that many would likely have to pay more for needed medications in future years. The House budget would also end Medicare as we know it, replacing guaranteed access to the traditional Medicare program with a voucher program, risking a death spiral in traditional Medicare.

Slash Investments in the Middle Class: Under the Republican budgets, both non-defense and base defense discretionary funding in 2016 would be at the lowest real levels in a decade. Compared to the President's Budget, if the Republican budgets were to take effect, these are just some of the impacts on Massachusetts:

- **Head Start:** 570 fewer children in Massachusetts would have access to Head Start services, representing a permanently missed opportunity to help these children enter elementary school ready to succeed.
- **Teachers and Schools:** Massachusetts would receive $19.6 million less funding for disadvantaged students, an amount that is enough to fund about 80 schools, 270 teacher and aide jobs, and 25,000 students.

- **Education for Children with Disabilities:** Massachusetts would receive $7.9 million less funding to provide educational opportunities for students with disabilities, representing an approximately 2.8 percent cut and shifting the burden for meeting these children's needs to Massachusetts and its local communities.
- **Job Training and Employment Services:** 46,200 fewer Massachusetts residents would receive job training and employment services, including help finding jobs and skills training.
- **Affordable Housing**: Massachusetts would receive approximately $84.2 million less in Federal funding, resulting in 5,010 fewer families receiving Housing Choice Vouchers, which enable very low-income families to afford decent, safe, and sanitary housing in the private market.
- **National Parks:** Construction and renovation projects would be prevented or delayed at six national parks in Massachusetts: Adams National Historical Park, Boston National Historical Park, Cape Cod National Seashore, Lowell National Historical Park, Minute Man National Historical Park, and Salem Maritime National Historic Site.

Balances Only with Gimmicks and Deep Cuts to Programs that Serve the Most Vulnerable and Help Expand Opportunity. On top of their cuts to middle-class investments and the ACA, the Republican budgets would cut:

- **Pell Grants:** Republican reductions to Pell would reduce financial aid for the 131,000 Massachusetts students who rely on Pell grants to afford college.
- **Medicaid:** The House Republican proposal to block grant Medicaid would cut Federal funding to Massachusetts by approximately $24 billion over ten years, impacting children, seniors, and people with disabilities who rely on Medicaid.
- **Supplemental Nutrition Assistance Program (SNAP):** House Republican proposals to block grant and slash SNAP would cut nutrition aid in Massachusetts by an estimated $2 billion over a five year period (2021-2025), jeopardizing nutrition assistance for the 863,000 Massachusetts residents who receive SNAP to help them put food on the table.

Fails to Address Our Crumbling Infrastructure: Republican budgets lack a real plan to address the looming expiration and insolvency of the Highway Trust Fund. Through the Highway Trust Fund, in FY 2014 the Federal Government obligated $638.6 million to Massachusetts through the Federal Aid Highways program for highway planning and construction and over $425.4 million through Transit Formula Grants that support our Nation's mass transit systems.

###

i. Numbers are rounded. For a description of how impacts were calculated, see http://go.wh.gov/RoNU1j

FOR IMMEDIATE RELEASE
March 24, 2015

FACT SHEET: Republican Budget Resolutions: Same Failed Top-Down Economics for Michigan

With more than 12 million private-sector jobs created over the last 60 months, it is clear that the President's middle class economic agenda is working. But instead of taking the steps we need to strengthen the standing of working families, the Republican budgets for fiscal year (FY) 2016 would return our economy to the same top-down economics that has failed us before: cutting taxes for millionaires and billionaires, while slashing investments in the middle class that we need to grow the economy, like education, job training, and manufacturing. The Republican proposals stand in stark contrast to the President's FY 2016 Budget, which would bring middle class economics into the 21st Century. A state-by-state breakdown of this contrast, including how the Republican budgets affect Michigan, can be found in a report released today here: http://go.wh.gov/RoNU1j.

The President's Budget builds on the progress we've made and shows what we can do if we invest in America's future and commit to an economy that rewards hard work, generates rising incomes, and allows everyone to share in the prosperity of a growing America. It lays out a strategy to strengthen our middle class and help America's hard-working families get ahead in a time of relentless economic and technological change. And it makes the critical investments needed to accelerate and sustain economic growth in the long run, including in research, education, training, and infrastructure.

Republicans have chosen different priorities. Yet again, they are seeking to balance the budget on the backs of the middle class, while cutting taxes for the wealthy and well-connected. They still won't say where many of their spending cuts come from. But they are clear that their budgets would continue the harmful cuts known as sequestration in 2016, threatening economic growth, cutting programs middle-class families count on, and attempting to fund national security through irresponsible budget gimmicks. Their budgets slash domestic investments that support the middle-class even more significantly after 2016, along with programs that serve the most vulnerable Americans. House Republicans would end Medicare as we know it, transforming it from a guarantee seniors can count on into a voucher program. After five years of the Affordable Care Act, more than 16 million people have gained coverage. Yet once again, the Republican budgets propose to repeal the Affordable Care Act's coverage expansions.

The choice could not be more clear or the consequences more stark. Thanks to President Obama and the resilience of the American people, the economy is growing

again. The Republican budgets would put that growth at risk and limit opportunity for the middle-class and those seeking to join it.

In Michigan, the Republican budgets would[i]:

Cut Taxes for Millionaires and Raise Taxes for Working Families and Students: While claiming to prioritize fiscal responsibility, the Republican budgets would not ask the wealthy to contribute a single dollar to deficit reduction, and the proposals specified in the House budget would cut taxes for millionaires by an average of at least $50,000. Meanwhile, the Republican budgets do nothing to prevent tax increases averaging $1,100 for 12 million families and students paying for college and $900 for 16 million working families with children. In 2015, 472,000 Michigan families will receive a total of $429 million in tax cuts from improvements to pro-work tax credits that would expire after 2017 under the Republican budgets.

Eliminate Affordable Health Care: The Affordable Care Act is working. After five years of the Affordable Care Act, more than 16 million people have gained coverage. Yet once again, the Republican budgets propose to repeal the Affordable Care Act's coverage expansions, taking away health insurance from millions of people. In particular, the Republican budgets would eliminate coverage for 341,000 Michigan residents who have newly signed up for coverage or re-enrolled through the Marketplaces. Some of these individuals would become uninsured while others would end up with worse or less affordable coverage.

Raise Health Care Costs for Seniors: 205,200 Michigan seniors and people with disabilities benefited by an average of $1,050 from the closure of the Medicare Part D prescription drug donut hole in 2014 alone. Under the Republican plan to repeal the Affordable Care Act, at least that many would likely have to pay more for needed medications in future years. The House budget would also end Medicare as we know it, replacing guaranteed access to the traditional Medicare program with a voucher program, risking a death spiral in traditional Medicare.

Slash Investments in the Middle Class: Under the Republican budgets, both non-defense and base defense discretionary funding in 2016 would be at the lowest real levels in a decade. Compared to the President's Budget, if the Republican budgets were to take effect, these are just some of the impacts on Michigan:

- **Head Start:** 1,240 fewer children in Michigan would have access to Head Start services, representing a permanently missed opportunity to help these children enter elementary school ready to succeed.
- **Teachers and Schools:** Michigan would receive $32.5 million less funding for disadvantaged students, an amount that is enough to fund about 120 schools, 450 teacher and aide jobs, and 39,000 students.

- **Education for Children with Disabilities:** Michigan would receive $11.5 million less funding to provide educational opportunities for students with disabilities, representing an approximately 2.9 percent cut and shifting the burden for meeting these children's needs to Michigan and its local communities.
- **Job Training and Employment Services:** 71,600 fewer Michigan residents would receive job training and employment services, including help finding jobs and skills training.
- **Affordable Housing:** Michigan would receive approximately $33.2 million less in Federal funding, resulting in 3,200 fewer families receiving Housing Choice Vouchers, which enable very low-income families to afford decent, safe, and sanitary housing in the private market.
- **National Parks:** Construction and renovation projects would be prevented or delayed at three national parks in Michigan: Isle Royal National Park, Keweenaw National Historical Park, and Sleeping Bear Dunes National Lakeshore.

Balances Only with Gimmicks and Deep Cuts to Programs that Serve the Most Vulnerable and Help Expand Opportunity. On top of their cuts to middle-class investments and the ACA, the Republican budgets would cut:

- **Pell Grants:** Republican reductions to Pell would reduce financial aid for the 269,000 Michigan students who rely on Pell grants to afford college.
- **Medicaid:** The House Republican proposal to block grant Medicaid would cut Federal funding to Michigan by approximately $30.1 billion over ten years, impacting children, seniors, and people with disabilities who rely on Medicaid.
- **Supplemental Nutrition Assistance Program (SNAP):** House Republican proposals to block grant and slash SNAP would cut nutrition aid in Michigan by an estimated $4.1 billion over a five year period (2021-2025), jeopardizing nutrition assistance for the 1,679,000 Michigan residents who receive SNAP to help them put food on the table.

Fails to Address Our Crumbling Infrastructure: Republican budgets lack a real plan to address the looming expiration and insolvency of the Highway Trust Fund. Through the Highway Trust Fund, in FY 2014 the Federal Government obligated $1.0 billion to Michigan through the Federal Aid Highways program for highway planning and construction and over $210.2 million through Transit Formula Grants that support our Nation's mass transit systems.

i. Numbers are rounded. For a description of how impacts were calculated, see http://go.wh.gov/RoNU1j

FOR IMMEDIATE RELEASE
March 24, 2015

FACT SHEET: Republican Budget Resolutions: Same Failed Top-Down Economics for Minnesota

With more than 12 million private-sector jobs created over the last 60 months, it is clear that the President's middle class economic agenda is working. But instead of taking the steps we need to strengthen the standing of working families, the Republican budgets for fiscal year (FY) 2016 would return our economy to the same top-down economics that has failed us before: cutting taxes for millionaires and billionaires, while slashing investments in the middle class that we need to grow the economy, like education, job training, and manufacturing. The Republican proposals stand in stark contrast to the President's FY 2016 Budget, which would bring middle class economics into the 21st Century. A state-by-state breakdown of this contrast, including how the Republican budgets affect Minnesota, can be found in a report released today here: http://go.wh.gov/RoNU1j.

The President's Budget builds on the progress we've made and shows what we can do if we invest in America's future and commit to an economy that rewards hard work, generates rising incomes, and allows everyone to share in the prosperity of a growing America. It lays out a strategy to strengthen our middle class and help America's hard-working families get ahead in a time of relentless economic and technological change. And it makes the critical investments needed to accelerate and sustain economic growth in the long run, including in research, education, training, and infrastructure.

Republicans have chosen different priorities. Yet again, they are seeking to balance the budget on the backs of the middle class, while cutting taxes for the wealthy and well-connected. They still won't say where many of their spending cuts come from. But they are clear that their budgets would continue the harmful cuts known as sequestration in 2016, threatening economic growth, cutting programs middle-class families count on, and attempting to fund national security through irresponsible budget gimmicks. Their budgets slash domestic investments that support the middle-class even more significantly after 2016, along with programs that serve the most vulnerable Americans. House Republicans would end Medicare as we know it, transforming it from a guarantee seniors can count on into a voucher program. After five years of the Affordable Care Act, more than 16 million people have gained coverage. Yet once again, the Republican budgets propose to repeal the Affordable Care Act's coverage expansions.

The choice could not be more clear or the consequences more stark. Thanks to President Obama and the resilience of the American people, the economy is growing

again. The Republican budgets would put that growth at risk and limit opportunity for the middle-class and those seeking to join it.

In Minnesota, the Republican budgets would[i]:

Cut Taxes for Millionaires and Raise Taxes for Working Families and Students: While claiming to prioritize fiscal responsibility, the Republican budgets would not ask the wealthy to contribute a single dollar to deficit reduction, and the proposals specified in the House budget would cut taxes for millionaires by an average of at least $50,000. Meanwhile, the Republican budgets do nothing to prevent tax increases averaging $1,100 for 12 million families and students paying for college and $900 for 16 million working families with children. In 2015, 191,000 Minnesota families will receive a total of $169 million in tax cuts from improvements to pro-work tax credits that would expire after 2017 under the Republican budgets.

Eliminate Affordable Health Care: The Affordable Care Act is working. After five years of the Affordable Care Act, more than 16 million people have gained coverage. Yet once again, the Republican budgets propose to repeal the Affordable Care Act's coverage expansions, taking away health insurance from millions of people. In particular, the Republican budgets would eliminate coverage for 60,000 Minnesota residents who have newly signed up for coverage or re-enrolled through the Marketplaces. Some of these individuals would become uninsured while others would end up with worse or less affordable coverage.

Raise Health Care Costs for Seniors: 69,200 Minnesota seniors and people with disabilities benefited by an average of $860 from the closure of the Medicare Part D prescription drug donut hole in 2014 alone. Under the Republican plan to repeal the Affordable Care Act, at least that many would likely have to pay more for needed medications in future years. The House budget would also end Medicare as we know it, replacing guaranteed access to the traditional Medicare program with a voucher program, risking a death spiral in traditional Medicare.

Slash Investments in the Middle Class: Under the Republican budgets, both non-defense and base defense discretionary funding in 2016 would be at the lowest real levels in a decade. Compared to the President's Budget, if the Republican budgets were to take effect, these are just some of the impacts on Minnesota:

- **Head Start:** 390 fewer children in Minnesota would have access to Head Start services, representing a permanently missed opportunity to help these children enter elementary school ready to succeed.
- **Teachers and Schools:** Minnesota would receive $12.5 million less funding for disadvantaged students, an amount that is enough to fund about 70 schools, 170 teacher and aide jobs, and 16,000 students.

- **Education for Children with Disabilities:** Minnesota would receive $5.3 million less funding to provide educational opportunities for students with disabilities, representing an approximately 2.8 percent cut and shifting the burden for meeting these children's needs to Minnesota and its local communities.
- **Job Training and Employment Services:** 37,200 fewer Minnesota residents would receive job training and employment services, including help finding jobs and skills training.
- **Affordable Housing**: Minnesota would receive approximately $21.3 million less in Federal funding, resulting in 1,940 fewer families receiving Housing Choice Vouchers, which enable very low-income families to afford decent, safe, and sanitary housing in the private market.
- **National Parks:** Construction and renovation projects would be prevented or delayed at Voyageurs National Park.

Balances Only with Gimmicks and Deep Cuts to Programs that Serve the Most Vulnerable and Help Expand Opportunity. On top of their cuts to middle-class investments and the ACA, the Republican budgets would cut:

- **Pell Grants:** Republican reductions to Pell would reduce financial aid for the 146,000 Minnesota students who rely on Pell grants to afford college.
- **Medicaid:** The House Republican proposal to block grant Medicaid would cut Federal funding to Minnesota by approximately $17.7 billion over ten years, impacting children, seniors, and people with disabilities who rely on Medicaid.
- **Supplemental Nutrition Assistance Program (SNAP):** House Republican proposals to block grant and slash SNAP would cut nutrition aid in Minnesota by an estimated $1.1 billion over a five year period (2021-2025), jeopardizing nutrition assistance for the 534,000 Minnesota residents who receive SNAP to help them put food on the table.

Fails to Address Our Crumbling Infrastructure: Republican budgets lack a real plan to address the looming expiration and insolvency of the Highway Trust Fund. Through the Highway Trust Fund, in FY 2014 the Federal Government obligated $654.1 million to Minnesota through the Federal Aid Highways program for highway planning and construction and over $191.7 million through Transit Formula Grants that support our Nation's mass transit systems.

i. Numbers are rounded. For a description of how impacts were calculated, see http://go.wh.gov/RoNU1j

FOR IMMEDIATE RELEASE
March 24, 2015

FACT SHEET: Republican Budget Resolutions: Same Failed Top-Down Economics for Mississippi

With more than 12 million private-sector jobs created over the last 60 months, it is clear that the President's middle class economic agenda is working. But instead of taking the steps we need to strengthen the standing of working families, the Republican budgets for fiscal year (FY) 2016 would return our economy to the same top-down economics that has failed us before: cutting taxes for millionaires and billionaires, while slashing investments in the middle class that we need to grow the economy, like education, job training, and manufacturing. The Republican proposals stand in stark contrast to the President's FY 2016 Budget, which would bring middle class economics into the 21st Century. A state-by-state breakdown of this contrast, including how the Republican budgets affect Mississippi, can be found in a report released today here: http://go.wh.gov/RoNU1j.

The President's Budget builds on the progress we've made and shows what we can do if we invest in America's future and commit to an economy that rewards hard work, generates rising incomes, and allows everyone to share in the prosperity of a growing America. It lays out a strategy to strengthen our middle class and help America's hard-working families get ahead in a time of relentless economic and technological change. And it makes the critical investments needed to accelerate and sustain economic growth in the long run, including in research, education, training, and infrastructure.

Republicans have chosen different priorities. Yet again, they are seeking to balance the budget on the backs of the middle class, while cutting taxes for the wealthy and well-connected. They still won't say where many of their spending cuts come from. But they are clear that their budgets would continue the harmful cuts known as sequestration in 2016, threatening economic growth, cutting programs middle-class families count on, and attempting to fund national security through irresponsible budget gimmicks. Their budgets slash domestic investments that support the middle-class even more significantly after 2016, along with programs that serve the most vulnerable Americans. House Republicans would end Medicare as we know it, transforming it from a guarantee seniors can count on into a voucher program. After five years of the Affordable Care Act, more than 16 million people have gained coverage. Yet once again, the Republican budgets propose to repeal the Affordable Care Act's coverage expansions.

The choice could not be more clear or the consequences more stark. Thanks to President Obama and the resilience of the American people, the economy is growing

again. The Republican budgets would put that growth at risk and limit opportunity for the middle-class and those seeking to join it.

In Mississippi, the Republican budgets would[i]:

Cut Taxes for Millionaires and Raise Taxes for Working Families and Students: While claiming to prioritize fiscal responsibility, the Republican budgets would not ask the wealthy to contribute a single dollar to deficit reduction, and the proposals specified in the House budget would cut taxes for millionaires by an average of at least $50,000. Meanwhile, the Republican budgets do nothing to prevent tax increases averaging $1,100 for 12 million families and students paying for college and $900 for 16 million working families with children. In 2015, 217,000 Mississippi families will receive a total of $202 million in tax cuts from improvements to pro-work tax credits that would expire after 2017 under the Republican budgets.

Eliminate Affordable Health Care: The Affordable Care Act is working. After five years of the Affordable Care Act, more than 16 million people have gained coverage. Yet once again, the Republican budgets propose to repeal the Affordable Care Act's coverage expansions, taking away health insurance from millions of people. In particular, the Republican budgets would eliminate coverage for 105,000 Mississippi residents who have newly signed up for coverage or re-enrolled through the Marketplaces. Some of these individuals would become uninsured while others would end up with worse or less affordable coverage.

Raise Health Care Costs for Seniors: 41,400 Mississippi seniors and people with disabilities benefited by an average of $750 from the closure of the Medicare Part D prescription drug donut hole in 2014 alone. Under the Republican plan to repeal the Affordable Care Act, at least that many would likely have to pay more for needed medications in future years. The House budget would also end Medicare as we know it, replacing guaranteed access to the traditional Medicare program with a voucher program, risking a death spiral in traditional Medicare.

Slash Investments in the Middle Class: Under the Republican budgets, both non-defense and base defense discretionary funding in 2016 would be at the lowest real levels in a decade. Compared to the President's Budget, if the Republican budgets were to take effect, these are just some of the impacts on Mississippi:

- **Head Start:** 840 fewer children in Mississippi would have access to Head Start services, representing a permanently missed opportunity to help these children enter elementary school ready to succeed.
- **Teachers and Schools:** Mississippi would receive $14.9 million less funding for disadvantaged students, an amount that is enough to fund about 50 schools, 200 teacher and aide jobs, and 27,000 students.

- **Education for Children with Disabilities:** Mississippi would receive $3.5 million less funding to provide educational opportunities for students with disabilities, representing an approximately 2.9 percent cut and shifting the burden for meeting these children's needs to Mississippi and its local communities.
- **Job Training and Employment Services:** 19,100 fewer Mississippi residents would receive job training and employment services, including help finding jobs and skills training.
- **Affordable Housing**: Mississippi would receive approximately $13.2 million less in Federal funding, resulting in 1,360 fewer families receiving Housing Choice Vouchers, which enable very low-income families to afford decent, safe, and sanitary housing in the private market.
- **National Parks:** Construction and renovation projects would be prevented or delayed at two national parks in Mississippi: Gulf Islands National Seashore and Vicksburg National Military Park.

Balances Only with Gimmicks and Deep Cuts to Programs that Serve the Most Vulnerable and Help Expand Opportunity. On top of their cuts to middle-class investments and the ACA, the Republican budgets would cut:

- **Pell Grants:** Republican reductions to Pell would reduce financial aid for the 99,000 Mississippi students who rely on Pell grants to afford college.
- **Medicaid:** The House Republican proposal to block grant Medicaid would cut Federal funding to Mississippi by approximately $11.4 billion over ten years, impacting children, seniors, and people with disabilities who rely on Medicaid.
- **Supplemental Nutrition Assistance Program (SNAP):** House Republican proposals to block grant and slash SNAP would cut nutrition aid in Mississippi by an estimated $1.4 billion over a five year period (2021-2025), jeopardizing nutrition assistance for the 657,000 Mississippi residents who receive SNAP to help them put food on the table.

Fails to Address Our Crumbling Infrastructure: Republican budgets lack a real plan to address the looming expiration and insolvency of the Highway Trust Fund. Through the Highway Trust Fund, in FY 2014 the Federal Government obligated $498.6 million to Mississippi through the Federal Aid Highways program for highway planning and construction and over $10.8 million through Transit Formula Grants that support our Nation's mass transit systems.

i. Numbers are rounded. For a description of how impacts were calculated, see http://go.wh.gov/RoNU1j

THE WHITE HOUSE

Office of the Press Secretary

FOR IMMEDIATE RELEASE

March 24, 2015

FACT SHEET: Republican Budget Resolutions: Same Failed Top-Down Economics for Missouri

With more than 12 million private-sector jobs created over the last 60 months, it is clear that the President's middle class economic agenda is working. But instead of taking the steps we need to strengthen the standing of working families, the Republican budgets for fiscal year (FY) 2016 would return our economy to the same top-down economics that has failed us before: cutting taxes for millionaires and billionaires, while slashing investments in the middle class that we need to grow the economy, like education, job training, and manufacturing. The Republican proposals stand in stark contrast to the President's FY 2016 Budget, which would bring middle class economics into the 21st Century. A state-by-state breakdown of this contrast, including how the Republican budgets affect Missouri, can be found in a report released today here: http://go.wh.gov/RoNU1j.

The President's Budget builds on the progress we've made and shows what we can do if we invest in America's future and commit to an economy that rewards hard work, generates rising incomes, and allows everyone to share in the prosperity of a growing America. It lays out a strategy to strengthen our middle class and help America's hard-working families get ahead in a time of relentless economic and technological change. And it makes the critical investments needed to accelerate and sustain economic growth in the long run, including in research, education, training, and infrastructure.

Republicans have chosen different priorities. Yet again, they are seeking to balance the budget on the backs of the middle class, while cutting taxes for the wealthy and well-connected. They still won't say where many of their spending cuts come from. But they are clear that their budgets would continue the harmful cuts known as sequestration in 2016, threatening economic growth, cutting programs middle-class families count on, and attempting to fund national security through irresponsible budget gimmicks. Their budgets slash domestic investments that support the middle-class even more significantly after 2016, along with programs that serve the most vulnerable Americans. House Republicans would end Medicare as we know it, transforming it from a guarantee seniors can count on into a voucher program. After five years of the Affordable Care Act, more than 16 million people have gained coverage. Yet once again, the Republican budgets propose to repeal the Affordable Care Act's coverage expansions.

The choice could not be more clear or the consequences more stark. Thanks to President Obama and the resilience of the American people, the economy is growing

again. The Republican budgets would put that growth at risk and limit opportunity for the middle-class and those seeking to join it.

In Missouri, the Republican budgets would[i]:

Cut Taxes for Millionaires and Raise Taxes for Working Families and Students: While claiming to prioritize fiscal responsibility, the Republican budgets would not ask the wealthy to contribute a single dollar to deficit reduction, and the proposals specified in the House budget would cut taxes for millionaires by an average of at least $50,000. Meanwhile, the Republican budgets do nothing to prevent tax increases averaging $1,100 for 12 million families and students paying for college and $900 for 16 million working families with children. In 2015, 296,000 Missouri families will receive a total of $265 million in tax cuts from improvements to pro-work tax credits that would expire after 2017 under the Republican budgets.

Eliminate Affordable Health Care: The Affordable Care Act is working. After five years of the Affordable Care Act, more than 16 million people have gained coverage. Yet once again, the Republican budgets propose to repeal the Affordable Care Act's coverage expansions, taking away health insurance from millions of people. In particular, the Republican budgets would eliminate coverage for 253,000 Missouri residents who have newly signed up for coverage or re-enrolled through the Marketplaces. Some of these individuals would become uninsured while others would end up with worse or less affordable coverage.

Raise Health Care Costs for Seniors: 109,000 Missouri seniors and people with disabilities benefited by an average of $870 from the closure of the Medicare Part D prescription drug donut hole in 2014 alone. Under the Republican plan to repeal the Affordable Care Act, at least that many would likely have to pay more for needed medications in future years. The House budget would also end Medicare as we know it, replacing guaranteed access to the traditional Medicare program with a voucher program, risking a death spiral in traditional Medicare.

Slash Investments in the Middle Class: Under the Republican budgets, both non-defense and base defense discretionary funding in 2016 would be at the lowest real levels in a decade. Compared to the President's Budget, if the Republican budgets were to take effect, these are just some of the impacts on Missouri:

- **Head Start:** 650 fewer children in Missouri would have access to Head Start services, representing a permanently missed opportunity to help these children enter elementary school ready to succeed.
- **Teachers and Schools:** Missouri would receive $18.6 million less funding for disadvantaged students, an amount that is enough to fund about 80 schools, 260 teacher and aide jobs, and 26,000 students.

- **Education for Children with Disabilities:** Missouri would receive $6.3 million less funding to provide educational opportunities for students with disabilities, representing an approximately 2.8 percent cut and shifting the burden for meeting these children's needs to Missouri and its local communities.
- **Job Training and Employment Services:** 40,700 fewer Missouri residents would receive job training and employment services, including help finding jobs and skills training.
- **Affordable Housing:** Missouri would receive approximately $22.8 million less in Federal funding, resulting in 2,360 fewer families receiving Housing Choice Vouchers, which enable very low-income families to afford decent, safe, and sanitary housing in the private market.
- **National Parks:** Construction and renovation projects would be prevented or delayed at Ozark National Scenic Riverways.

Balances Only with Gimmicks and Deep Cuts to Programs that Serve the Most Vulnerable and Help Expand Opportunity. On top of their cuts to middle-class investments and the ACA, the Republican budgets would cut:

- **Pell Grants:** Republican reductions to Pell would reduce financial aid for the 165,000 Missouri students who rely on Pell grants to afford college.
- **Medicaid:** The House Republican proposal to block grant Medicaid would cut Federal funding to Missouri by approximately $18.0 billion over ten years, impacting children, seniors, and people with disabilities who rely on Medicaid.
- **Supplemental Nutrition Assistance Program (SNAP):** House Republican proposals to block grant and slash SNAP would cut nutrition aid in Missouri by an estimated $2 billion over a five year period (2021-2025), jeopardizing nutrition assistance for the 858,000 Missouri residents who receive SNAP to help them put food on the table.

Fails to Address Our Crumbling Infrastructure: Republican budgets lack a real plan to address the looming expiration and insolvency of the Highway Trust Fund. Through the Highway Trust Fund, in FY 2014 the Federal Government obligated $928.6 million to Missouri through the Federal Aid Highways program for highway planning and construction and over $162.6 million through Transit Formula Grants that support our Nation's mass transit systems.

###

i. Numbers are rounded. For a description of how impacts were calculated, see http://go.wh.gov/RoNU1j

FOR IMMEDIATE RELEASE
March 24, 2015

FACT SHEET: Republican Budget Resolutions: Same Failed Top-Down Economics for Montana

With more than 12 million private-sector jobs created over the last 60 months, it is clear that the President's middle class economic agenda is working. But instead of taking the steps we need to strengthen the standing of working families, the Republican budgets for fiscal year (FY) 2016 would return our economy to the same top-down economics that has failed us before: cutting taxes for millionaires and billionaires, while slashing investments in the middle class that we need to grow the economy, like education, job training, and manufacturing. The Republican proposals stand in stark contrast to the President's FY 2016 Budget, which would bring middle class economics into the 21st Century. A state-by-state breakdown of this contrast, including how the Republican budgets affect Montana, can be found in a report released today here: http://go.wh.gov/RoNU1j.

The President's Budget builds on the progress we've made and shows what we can do if we invest in America's future and commit to an economy that rewards hard work, generates rising incomes, and allows everyone to share in the prosperity of a growing America. It lays out a strategy to strengthen our middle class and help America's hard-working families get ahead in a time of relentless economic and technological change. And it makes the critical investments needed to accelerate and sustain economic growth in the long run, including in research, education, training, and infrastructure.

Republicans have chosen different priorities. Yet again, they are seeking to balance the budget on the backs of the middle class, while cutting taxes for the wealthy and well-connected. They still won't say where many of their spending cuts come from. But they are clear that their budgets would continue the harmful cuts known as sequestration in 2016, threatening economic growth, cutting programs middle-class families count on, and attempting to fund national security through irresponsible budget gimmicks. Their budgets slash domestic investments that support the middle-class even more significantly after 2016, along with programs that serve the most vulnerable Americans. House Republicans would end Medicare as we know it, transforming it from a guarantee seniors can count on into a voucher program. After five years of the Affordable Care Act, more than 16 million people have gained coverage. Yet once again, the Republican budgets propose to repeal the Affordable Care Act's coverage expansions.

The choice could not be more clear or the consequences more stark. Thanks to President Obama and the resilience of the American people, the economy is growing

again. The Republican budgets would put that growth at risk and limit opportunity for the middle-class and those seeking to join it.

In Montana, the Republican budgets would[i]:

Cut Taxes for Millionaires and Raise Taxes for Working Families and Students: While claiming to prioritize fiscal responsibility, the Republican budgets would not ask the wealthy to contribute a single dollar to deficit reduction, and the proposals specified in the House budget would cut taxes for millionaires by an average of at least $50,000. Meanwhile, the Republican budgets do nothing to prevent tax increases averaging $1,100 for 12 million families and students paying for college and $900 for 16 million working families with children. In 2015, 47,000 Montana families will receive a total of $40 million in tax cuts from improvements to pro-work tax credits that would expire after 2017 under the Republican budgets.

Eliminate Affordable Health Care: The Affordable Care Act is working. After five years of the Affordable Care Act, more than 16 million people have gained coverage. Yet once again, the Republican budgets propose to repeal the Affordable Care Act's coverage expansions, taking away health insurance from millions of people. In particular, the Republican budgets would eliminate coverage for 54,000 Montana residents who have newly signed up for coverage or re-enrolled through the Marketplaces. Some of these individuals would become uninsured while others would end up with worse or less affordable coverage.

Raise Health Care Costs for Seniors: 13,100 Montana seniors and people with disabilities benefited by an average of $800 from the closure of the Medicare Part D prescription drug donut hole in 2014 alone. Under the Republican plan to repeal the Affordable Care Act, at least that many would likely have to pay more for needed medications in future years. The House budget would also end Medicare as we know it, replacing guaranteed access to the traditional Medicare program with a voucher program, risking a death spiral in traditional Medicare.

Slash Investments in the Middle Class: Under the Republican budgets, both non-defense and base defense discretionary funding in 2016 would be at the lowest real levels in a decade. Compared to the President's Budget, if the Republican budgets were to take effect, these are just some of the impacts on Montana:

- **Head Start:** 110 fewer children in Montana would have access to Head Start services, representing a permanently missed opportunity to help these children enter elementary school ready to succeed.
- **Teachers and Schools:** Montana would receive $4.2 million less funding for disadvantaged students, an amount that is enough to fund about 60 schools, 60 teacher and aide jobs, and 5,000 students.

- **Education for Children with Disabilities:** Montana would receive $1.2 million less funding to provide educational opportunities for students with disabilities, representing an approximately 3.1 percent cut and shifting the burden for meeting these children's needs to Montana and its local communities.
- **Job Training and Employment Services:** 16,700 fewer Montana residents would receive job training and employment services, including help finding jobs and skills training.
- **Affordable Housing**: Montana would receive approximately $2.9 million less in Federal funding, resulting in 310 fewer families receiving Housing Choice Vouchers, which enable very low-income families to afford decent, safe, and sanitary housing in the private market.
- **National Parks:** Construction and renovation projects would be prevented or delayed at three national parks in Montana: Bighorn Canyon National Recreation Area, Glacier National Park, and Bighorn Canyon National Recreation Area.

Balances Only with Gimmicks and Deep Cuts to Programs that Serve the Most Vulnerable and Help Expand Opportunity. On top of their cuts to middle-class investments and the ACA, the Republican budgets would cut:

- **Pell Grants:** Republican reductions to Pell would reduce financial aid for the 22,000 Montana students who rely on Pell grants to afford college.
- **Medicaid:** The House Republican proposal to block grant Medicaid would cut Federal funding to Montana by approximately $2.4 billion over ten years, impacting children, seniors, and people with disabilities who rely on Medicaid.
- **Supplemental Nutrition Assistance Program (SNAP):** House Republican proposals to block grant and slash SNAP would cut nutrition aid in Montana by an estimated $300 million over a five year period (2021-2025), jeopardizing nutrition assistance for the 125,000 Montana residents who receive SNAP to help them put food on the table.

Fails to Address Our Crumbling Infrastructure: Republican budgets lack a real plan to address the looming expiration and insolvency of the Highway Trust Fund. Through the Highway Trust Fund, in FY 2014 the Federal Government obligated $386.2 million to Montana through the Federal Aid Highways program for highway planning and construction and over $26.5 million through Transit Formula Grants that support our Nation's mass transit systems.

###

i. Numbers are rounded. For a description of how impacts were calculated, see http://go.wh.gov/RoNU1j

THE WHITE HOUSE
Office of the Press Secretary

FOR IMMEDIATE RELEASE
March 24, 2015

**FACT SHEET: Republican Budget Resolutions: Same Failed Top-Down Economics
for Nebraska**

With more than 12 million private-sector jobs created over the last 60 months, it is clear
that the President's middle class economic agenda is working. But instead of taking the
steps we need to strengthen the standing of working families, the Republican budgets
for fiscal year (FY) 2016 would return our economy to the same top-down economics
that has failed us before: cutting taxes for millionaires and billionaires, while slashing
investments in the middle class that we need to grow the economy, like education, job
training, and manufacturing. The Republican proposals stand in stark contrast to the
President's FY 2016 Budget, which would bring middle class economics into the 21st
Century. A state-by-state breakdown of this contrast, including how the Republican
budgets affect Nebraska, can be found in a report released today here:
http://go.wh.gov/RoNU1j.

The President's Budget builds on the progress we've made and shows what we can do
if we invest in America's future and commit to an economy that rewards hard work,
generates rising incomes, and allows everyone to share in the prosperity of a growing
America. It lays out a strategy to strengthen our middle class and help America's hard-
working families get ahead in a time of relentless economic and technological change.
And it makes the critical investments needed to accelerate and sustain economic growth
in the long run, including in research, education, training, and infrastructure.

Republicans have chosen different priorities. Yet again, they are seeking to balance the
budget on the backs of the middle class, while cutting taxes for the wealthy and well-
connected. They still won't say where many of their spending cuts come from. But
they are clear that their budgets would continue the harmful cuts known as
sequestration in 2016, threatening economic growth, cutting programs middle-class
families count on, and attempting to fund national security through irresponsible
budget gimmicks. Their budgets slash domestic investments that support the middle-
class even more significantly after 2016, along with programs that serve the most
vulnerable Americans. House Republicans would end Medicare as we know it,
transforming it from a guarantee seniors can count on into a voucher program. After
five years of the Affordable Care Act, more than 16 million people have gained
coverage. Yet once again, the Republican budgets propose to repeal the Affordable
Care Act's coverage expansions.

The choice could not be more clear or the consequences more stark. Thanks to
President Obama and the resilience of the American people, the economy is growing

again. The Republican budgets would put that growth at risk and limit opportunity for the middle-class and those seeking to join it.

In Nebraska, the Republican budgets would[i]:

Cut Taxes for Millionaires and Raise Taxes for Working Families and Students: While claiming to prioritize fiscal responsibility, the Republican budgets would not ask the wealthy to contribute a single dollar to deficit reduction, and the proposals specified in the House budget would cut taxes for millionaires by an average of at least $50,000. Meanwhile, the Republican budgets do nothing to prevent tax increases averaging $1,100 for 12 million families and students paying for college and $900 for 16 million working families with children. In 2015, 81,000 Nebraska families will receive a total of $73 million in tax cuts from improvements to pro-work tax credits that would expire after 2017 under the Republican budgets.

Eliminate Affordable Health Care: The Affordable Care Act is working. After five years of the Affordable Care Act, more than 16 million people have gained coverage. Yet once again, the Republican budgets propose to repeal the Affordable Care Act's coverage expansions, taking away health insurance from millions of people. In particular, the Republican budgets would eliminate coverage for 74,000 Nebraska residents who have newly signed up for coverage or re-enrolled through the Marketplaces. Some of these individuals would become uninsured while others would end up with worse or less affordable coverage.

Raise Health Care Costs for Seniors: 29,700 Nebraska seniors and people with disabilities benefited by an average of $800 from the closure of the Medicare Part D prescription drug donut hole in 2014 alone. Under the Republican plan to repeal the Affordable Care Act, at least that many would likely have to pay more for needed medications in future years. The House budget would also end Medicare as we know it, replacing guaranteed access to the traditional Medicare program with a voucher program, risking a death spiral in traditional Medicare.

Slash Investments in the Middle Class: Under the Republican budgets, both non-defense and base defense discretionary funding in 2016 would be at the lowest real levels in a decade. Compared to the President's Budget, if the Republican budgets were to take effect, these are just some of the impacts on Nebraska:

- **Head Start:** 200 fewer children in Nebraska would have access to Head Start services, representing a permanently missed opportunity to help these children enter elementary school ready to succeed.
- **Teachers and Schools:** Nebraska would receive $5.9 million less funding for disadvantaged students, an amount that is enough to fund about 40 schools, 80 teacher and aide jobs, and 9,000 students.

- **Education for Children with Disabilities:** Nebraska would receive $2.1 million less funding to provide educational opportunities for students with disabilities, representing an approximately 2.8 percent cut and shifting the burden for meeting these children's needs to Nebraska and its local communities.
- **Job Training and Employment Services:** 18,700 fewer Nebraska residents would receive job training and employment services, including help finding jobs and skills training.
- **Affordable Housing:** Nebraska would receive approximately $6.2 million less in Federal funding, resulting in 740 fewer families receiving Housing Choice Vouchers, which enable very low-income families to afford decent, safe, and sanitary housing in the private market.
- **National Parks:** Construction and renovation projects would be prevented or delayed at Scotts Bluff National Monument.

Balances Only with Gimmicks and Deep Cuts to Programs that Serve the Most Vulnerable and Help Expand Opportunity. On top of their cuts to middle-class investments and the ACA, the Republican budgets would cut:

- **Pell Grants:** Republican reductions to Pell would reduce financial aid for the 39,000 Nebraska students who rely on Pell grants to afford college.
- **Medicaid:** The House Republican proposal to block grant Medicaid would cut Federal funding to Nebraska by approximately $3.3 billion over ten years, impacting children, seniors, and people with disabilities who rely on Medicaid.
- **Supplemental Nutrition Assistance Program (SNAP):** House Republican proposals to block grant and slash SNAP would cut nutrition aid in Nebraska by an estimated $400 million over a five year period (2021-2025), jeopardizing nutrition assistance for the 174,000 Nebraska residents who receive SNAP to help them put food on the table.

Fails to Address Our Crumbling Infrastructure: Republican budgets lack a real plan to address the looming expiration and insolvency of the Highway Trust Fund. Through the Highway Trust Fund, in FY 2014 the Federal Government obligated $289.6 million to Nebraska through the Federal Aid Highways program for highway planning and construction and over $32.3 million through Transit Formula Grants that support our Nation's mass transit systems.

i. Numbers are rounded. For a description of how impacts were calculated, see http://go.wh.gov/RoNU1j

FOR IMMEDIATE RELEASE
March 24, 2015

FACT SHEET: Republican Budget Resolutions: Same Failed Top-Down Economics for Nevada

With more than 12 million private-sector jobs created over the last 60 months, it is clear that the President's middle class economic agenda is working. But instead of taking the steps we need to strengthen the standing of working families, the Republican budgets for fiscal year (FY) 2016 would return our economy to the same top-down economics that has failed us before: cutting taxes for millionaires and billionaires, while slashing investments in the middle class that we need to grow the economy, like education, job training, and manufacturing. The Republican proposals stand in stark contrast to the President's FY 2016 Budget, which would bring middle class economics into the 21st Century. A state-by-state breakdown of this contrast, including how the Republican budgets affect Nevada, can be found in a report released today here: http://go.wh.gov/RoNU1j.

The President's Budget builds on the progress we've made and shows what we can do if we invest in America's future and commit to an economy that rewards hard work, generates rising incomes, and allows everyone to share in the prosperity of a growing America. It lays out a strategy to strengthen our middle class and help America's hard-working families get ahead in a time of relentless economic and technological change. And it makes the critical investments needed to accelerate and sustain economic growth in the long run, including in research, education, training, and infrastructure.

Republicans have chosen different priorities. Yet again, they are seeking to balance the budget on the backs of the middle class, while cutting taxes for the wealthy and well-connected. They still won't say where many of their spending cuts come from. But they are clear that their budgets would continue the harmful cuts known as sequestration in 2016, threatening economic growth, cutting programs middle-class families count on, and attempting to fund national security through irresponsible budget gimmicks. Their budgets slash domestic investments that support the middle-class even more significantly after 2016, along with programs that serve the most vulnerable Americans. House Republicans would end Medicare as we know it, transforming it from a guarantee seniors can count on into a voucher program. After five years of the Affordable Care Act, more than 16 million people have gained coverage. Yet once again, the Republican budgets propose to repeal the Affordable Care Act's coverage expansions.

The choice could not be more clear or the consequences more stark. Thanks to President Obama and the resilience of the American people, the economy is growing

again. The Republican budgets would put that growth at risk and limit opportunity for the middle-class and those seeking to join it.

In Nevada, the Republican budgets would[i]:

Cut Taxes for Millionaires and Raise Taxes for Working Families and Students: While claiming to prioritize fiscal responsibility, the Republican budgets would not ask the wealthy to contribute a single dollar to deficit reduction, and the proposals specified in the House budget would cut taxes for millionaires by an average of at least $50,000. Meanwhile, the Republican budgets do nothing to prevent tax increases averaging $1,100 for 12 million families and students paying for college and $900 for 16 million working families with children. In 2015, 146,000 Nevada families will receive a total of $136 million in tax cuts from improvements to pro-work tax credits that would expire after 2017 under the Republican budgets.

Eliminate Affordable Health Care: The Affordable Care Act is working. After five years of the Affordable Care Act, more than 16 million people have gained coverage. Yet once again, the Republican budgets propose to repeal the Affordable Care Act's coverage expansions, taking away health insurance from millions of people. In particular, the Republican budgets would eliminate coverage for 74,000 Nevada residents who have newly signed up for coverage or re-enrolled through the Marketplaces. Some of these individuals would become uninsured while others would end up with worse or less affordable coverage.

Raise Health Care Costs for Seniors: 33,000 Nevada seniors and people with disabilities benefited by an average of $870 from the closure of the Medicare Part D prescription drug donut hole in 2014 alone. Under the Republican plan to repeal the Affordable Care Act, at least that many would likely have to pay more for needed medications in future years. The House budget would also end Medicare as we know it, replacing guaranteed access to the traditional Medicare program with a voucher program, risking a death spiral in traditional Medicare.

Slash Investments in the Middle Class: Under the Republican budgets, both non-defense and base defense discretionary funding in 2016 would be at the lowest real levels in a decade. Compared to the President's Budget, if the Republican budgets were to take effect, these are just some of the impacts on Nevada:

- **Head Start:** 130 fewer children in Nevada would have access to Head Start services, representing a permanently missed opportunity to help these children enter elementary school ready to succeed.
- **Teachers and Schools:** Nevada would receive $11.2 million less funding for disadvantaged students, an amount that is enough to fund about 20 schools, 150 teacher and aide jobs, and 22,000 students.

- **Education for Children with Disabilities:** Nevada would receive $3.3 million less funding to provide educational opportunities for students with disabilities, representing an approximately 4.5 percent cut and shifting the burden for meeting these children's needs to Nevada and its local communities.
- **Job Training and Employment Services:** 20,700 fewer Nevada residents would receive job training and employment services, including help finding jobs and skills training.
- **Affordable Housing**: Nevada would receive approximately $12.6 million less in Federal funding, resulting in 920 fewer families receiving Housing Choice Vouchers, which enable very low-income families to afford decent, safe, and sanitary housing in the private market.

Balances Only with Gimmicks and Deep Cuts to Programs that Serve the Most Vulnerable and Help Expand Opportunity. On top of their cuts to middle-class investments and the ACA, the Republican budgets would cut:

- **Pell Grants:** Republican reductions to Pell would reduce financial aid for the 35,000 Nevada students who rely on Pell grants to afford college.
- **Medicaid:** The House Republican proposal to block grant Medicaid would cut Federal funding to Nevada by approximately $5.3 billion over ten years, impacting children, seniors, and people with disabilities who rely on Medicaid.
- **Supplemental Nutrition Assistance Program (SNAP):** House Republican proposals to block grant and slash SNAP would cut nutrition aid in Nevada by an estimated $900 million over a five year period (2021-2025), jeopardizing nutrition assistance for the 384,000 Nevada residents who receive SNAP to help them put food on the table.

Fails to Address Our Crumbling Infrastructure: Republican budgets lack a real plan to address the looming expiration and insolvency of the Highway Trust Fund. Through the Highway Trust Fund, in FY 2014 the Federal Government obligated $338.5 million to Nevada through the Federal Aid Highways program for highway planning and construction and over $70.1 million through Transit Formula Grants that support our Nation's mass transit systems.

i. Numbers are rounded. For a description of how impacts were calculated, see http://go.wh.gov/RoNU1j

FOR IMMEDIATE RELEASE
March 24, 2015

FACT SHEET: Republican Budget Resolutions: Same Failed Top-Down Economics for New Hampshire

With more than 12 million private-sector jobs created over the last 60 months, it is clear that the President's middle class economic agenda is working. But instead of taking the steps we need to strengthen the standing of working families, the Republican budgets for fiscal year (FY) 2016 would return our economy to the same top-down economics that has failed us before: cutting taxes for millionaires and billionaires, while slashing investments in the middle class that we need to grow the economy, like education, job training, and manufacturing. The Republican proposals stand in stark contrast to the President's FY 2016 Budget, which would bring middle class economics into the 21st Century. A state-by-state breakdown of this contrast, including how the Republican budgets affect New Hampshire, can be found in a report released today here: http://go.wh.gov/RoNU1j.

The President's Budget builds on the progress we've made and shows what we can do if we invest in America's future and commit to an economy that rewards hard work, generates rising incomes, and allows everyone to share in the prosperity of a growing America. It lays out a strategy to strengthen our middle class and help America's hard-working families get ahead in a time of relentless economic and technological change. And it makes the critical investments needed to accelerate and sustain economic growth in the long run, including in research, education, training, and infrastructure.

Republicans have chosen different priorities. Yet again, they are seeking to balance the budget on the backs of the middle class, while cutting taxes for the wealthy and well-connected. They still won't say where many of their spending cuts come from. But they are clear that their budgets would continue the harmful cuts known as sequestration in 2016, threatening economic growth, cutting programs middle-class families count on, and attempting to fund national security through irresponsible budget gimmicks. Their budgets slash domestic investments that support the middle-class even more significantly after 2016, along with programs that serve the most vulnerable Americans. House Republicans would end Medicare as we know it, transforming it from a guarantee seniors can count on into a voucher program. After five years of the Affordable Care Act, more than 16 million people have gained coverage. Yet once again, the Republican budgets propose to repeal the Affordable Care Act's coverage expansions.

The choice could not be more clear or the consequences more stark. Thanks to President Obama and the resilience of the American people, the economy is growing

again. The Republican budgets would put that growth at risk and limit opportunity for the middle-class and those seeking to join it.

In New Hampshire, the Republican budgets would[i]:

Cut Taxes for Millionaires and Raise Taxes for Working Families and Students: While claiming to prioritize fiscal responsibility, the Republican budgets would not ask the wealthy to contribute a single dollar to deficit reduction, and the proposals specified in the House budget would cut taxes for millionaires by an average of at least $50,000. Meanwhile, the Republican budgets do nothing to prevent tax increases averaging $1,100 for 12 million families and students paying for college and $900 for 16 million working families with children. In 2015, 40,000 New Hampshire families will receive a total of $33 million in tax cuts from improvements to pro-work tax credits that would expire after 2017 under the Republican budgets.

Eliminate Affordable Health Care: The Affordable Care Act is working. After five years of the Affordable Care Act, more than 16 million people have gained coverage. Yet once again, the Republican budgets propose to repeal the Affordable Care Act's coverage expansions, taking away health insurance from millions of people. In particular, the Republican budgets would eliminate coverage for 53,000 New Hampshire residents who have newly signed up for coverage or re-enrolled through the Marketplaces. Some of these individuals would become uninsured while others would end up with worse or less affordable coverage.

Raise Health Care Costs for Seniors: 18,900 New Hampshire seniors and people with disabilities benefited by an average of $900 from the closure of the Medicare Part D prescription drug donut hole in 2014 alone. Under the Republican plan to repeal the Affordable Care Act, at least that many would likely have to pay more for needed medications in future years. The House budget would also end Medicare as we know it, replacing guaranteed access to the traditional Medicare program with a voucher program, risking a death spiral in traditional Medicare.

Slash Investments in the Middle Class: Under the Republican budgets, both non-defense and base defense discretionary funding in 2016 would be at the lowest real levels in a decade. Compared to the President's Budget, if the Republican budgets were to take effect, these are just some of the impacts on New Hampshire:

- **Head Start:** 70 fewer children in New Hampshire would have access to Head Start services, representing a permanently missed opportunity to help these children enter elementary school ready to succeed.
- **Teachers and Schools:** New Hampshire would receive $3.6 million less funding for disadvantaged students, an amount that is enough to fund about 20 schools, 50 teacher and aide jobs, and 2,000 students.

- **Education for Children with Disabilities:** New Hampshire would receive $1.3 million less funding to provide educational opportunities for students with disabilities, representing an approximately 2.8 percent cut and shifting the burden for meeting these children's needs to New Hampshire and its local communities.
- **Job Training and Employment Services:** 9,000 fewer New Hampshire residents would receive job training and employment services, including help finding jobs and skills training.
- **Affordable Housing:** New Hampshire would receive approximately $7.9 million less in Federal funding, resulting in 620 fewer families receiving Housing Choice Vouchers, which enable very low-income families to afford decent, safe, and sanitary housing in the private market.
- **National Parks:** Construction and renovation projects would be prevented or delayed at two national parks in New Hampshire: Appalachian National Scenic Trail and Saint-Gaudens National Historic Site.

Balances Only with Gimmicks and Deep Cuts to Programs that Serve the Most Vulnerable and Help Expand Opportunity. On top of their cuts to middle-class investments and the ACA, the Republican budgets would cut:

- **Pell Grants:** Republican reductions to Pell would reduce financial aid for the 23,000 New Hampshire students who rely on Pell grants to afford college.
- **Medicaid:** The House Republican proposal to block grant Medicaid would cut Federal funding to New Hampshire by approximately $2.3 billion over ten years, impacting children, seniors, and people with disabilities who rely on Medicaid.
- **Supplemental Nutrition Assistance Program (SNAP):** House Republican proposals to block grant and slash SNAP would cut nutrition aid in New Hampshire by an estimated $200 million over a five year period (2021-2025), jeopardizing nutrition assistance for the 112,000 New Hampshire residents who receive SNAP to help them put food on the table.

Fails to Address Our Crumbling Infrastructure: Republican budgets lack a real plan to address the looming expiration and insolvency of the Highway Trust Fund. Through the Highway Trust Fund, in FY 2014 the Federal Government obligated $167.3 million to New Hampshire through the Federal Aid Highways program for highway planning and construction and over $16.8 million through Transit Formula Grants that support our Nation's mass transit systems.

###

i. Numbers are rounded. For a description of how impacts were calculated, see http://go.wh.gov/RoNU1j

FOR IMMEDIATE RELEASE
March 24, 2015

FACT SHEET: Republican Budget Resolutions: Same Failed Top-Down Economics for New Jersey

With more than 12 million private-sector jobs created over the last 60 months, it is clear that the President's middle class economic agenda is working. But instead of taking the steps we need to strengthen the standing of working families, the Republican budgets for fiscal year (FY) 2016 would return our economy to the same top-down economics that has failed us before: cutting taxes for millionaires and billionaires, while slashing investments in the middle class that we need to grow the economy, like education, job training, and manufacturing. The Republican proposals stand in stark contrast to the President's FY 2016 Budget, which would bring middle class economics into the 21st Century. A state-by-state breakdown of this contrast, including how the Republican budgets affect New Jersey, can be found in a report released today here: http://go.wh.gov/RoNU1j.

The President's Budget builds on the progress we've made and shows what we can do if we invest in America's future and commit to an economy that rewards hard work, generates rising incomes, and allows everyone to share in the prosperity of a growing America. It lays out a strategy to strengthen our middle class and help America's hard-working families get ahead in a time of relentless economic and technological change. And it makes the critical investments needed to accelerate and sustain economic growth in the long run, including in research, education, training, and infrastructure.

Republicans have chosen different priorities. Yet again, they are seeking to balance the budget on the backs of the middle class, while cutting taxes for the wealthy and well-connected. They still won't say where many of their spending cuts come from. But they are clear that their budgets would continue the harmful cuts known as sequestration in 2016, threatening economic growth, cutting programs middle-class families count on, and attempting to fund national security through irresponsible budget gimmicks. Their budgets slash domestic investments that support the middle-class even more significantly after 2016, along with programs that serve the most vulnerable Americans. House Republicans would end Medicare as we know it, transforming it from a guarantee seniors can count on into a voucher program. After five years of the Affordable Care Act, more than 16 million people have gained coverage. Yet once again, the Republican budgets propose to repeal the Affordable Care Act's coverage expansions.

The choice could not be more clear or the consequences more stark. Thanks to President Obama and the resilience of the American people, the economy is growing

again. The Republican budgets would put that growth at risk and limit opportunity for the middle-class and those seeking to join it.

In New Jersey, the Republican budgets would[i]:

Cut Taxes for Millionaires and Raise Taxes for Working Families and Students: While claiming to prioritize fiscal responsibility, the Republican budgets would not ask the wealthy to contribute a single dollar to deficit reduction, and the proposals specified in the House budget would cut taxes for millionaires by an average of at least $50,000. Meanwhile, the Republican budgets do nothing to prevent tax increases averaging $1,100 for 12 million families and students paying for college and $900 for 16 million working families with children. In 2015, 333,000 New Jersey families will receive a total of $296 million in tax cuts from improvements to pro-work tax credits that would expire after 2017 under the Republican budgets.

Eliminate Affordable Health Care: The Affordable Care Act is working. After five years of the Affordable Care Act, more than 16 million people have gained coverage. Yet once again, the Republican budgets propose to repeal the Affordable Care Act's coverage expansions, taking away health insurance from millions of people. In particular, the Republican budgets would eliminate coverage for 254,000 New Jersey residents who have newly signed up for coverage or re-enrolled through the Marketplaces. Some of these individuals would become uninsured while others would end up with worse or less affordable coverage.

Raise Health Care Costs for Seniors: 214,300 New Jersey seniors and people with disabilities benefited by an average of $1,140 from the closure of the Medicare Part D prescription drug donut hole in 2014 alone. Under the Republican plan to repeal the Affordable Care Act, at least that many would likely have to pay more for needed medications in future years. The House budget would also end Medicare as we know it, replacing guaranteed access to the traditional Medicare program with a voucher program, risking a death spiral in traditional Medicare.

Slash Investments in the Middle Class: Under the Republican budgets, both non-defense and base defense discretionary funding in 2016 would be at the lowest real levels in a decade. Compared to the President's Budget, if the Republican budgets were to take effect, these are just some of the impacts on New Jersey:

- **Head Start:** 710 fewer children in New Jersey would have access to Head Start services, representing a permanently missed opportunity to help these children enter elementary school ready to succeed.
- **Teachers and Schools:** New Jersey would receive $28.6 million less funding for disadvantaged students, an amount that is enough to fund about 120 schools, 390 teacher and aide jobs, and 33,000 students.

- **Education for Children with Disabilities:** New Jersey would receive $10.0 million less funding to provide educational opportunities for students with disabilities, representing an approximately 2.8 percent cut and shifting the burden for meeting these children's needs to New Jersey and its local communities.
- **Job Training and Employment Services:** 64,600 fewer New Jersey residents would receive job training and employment services, including help finding jobs and skills training.
- **Affordable Housing**: New Jersey would receive approximately $68.7 million less in Federal funding, resulting in 4,050 fewer families receiving Housing Choice Vouchers, which enable very low-income families to afford decent, safe, and sanitary housing in the private market.
- **National Parks:** Construction and renovation projects would be prevented or delayed at two national parks in New Jersey: Thomas Edison National Historical Park and Appalachian National Scenic Trail.

Balances Only with Gimmicks and Deep Cuts to Programs that Serve the Most Vulnerable and Help Expand Opportunity. On top of their cuts to middle-class investments and the ACA, the Republican budgets would cut:

- **Pell Grants:** Republican reductions to Pell would reduce financial aid for the 173,000 New Jersey students who rely on Pell grants to afford college.
- **Medicaid:** The House Republican proposal to block grant Medicaid would cut Federal funding to New Jersey by approximately $23.2 billion over ten years, impacting children, seniors, and people with disabilities who rely on Medicaid.
- **Supplemental Nutrition Assistance Program (SNAP):** House Republican proposals to block grant and slash SNAP would cut nutrition aid in New Jersey by an estimated $2 billion over a five year period (2021-2025), jeopardizing nutrition assistance for the 883,000 New Jersey residents who receive SNAP to help them put food on the table.

Fails to Address Our Crumbling Infrastructure: Republican budgets lack a real plan to address the looming expiration and insolvency of the Highway Trust Fund. Through the Highway Trust Fund, in FY 2014 the Federal Government obligated $700.7 million to New Jersey through the Federal Aid Highways program for highway planning and construction and over $921.2 million through Transit Formula Grants that support our Nation's mass transit systems.

i. Numbers are rounded. For a description of how impacts were calculated, see http://go.wh.gov/RoNU1j

THE WHITE HOUSE
Office of the Press Secretary

FOR IMMEDIATE RELEASE
March 24, 2015

FACT SHEET: Republican Budget Resolutions: Same Failed Top-Down Economics for New Mexico

With more than 12 million private-sector jobs created over the last 60 months, it is clear that the President's middle class economic agenda is working. But instead of taking the steps we need to strengthen the standing of working families, the Republican budgets for fiscal year (FY) 2016 would return our economy to the same top-down economics that has failed us before: cutting taxes for millionaires and billionaires, while slashing investments in the middle class that we need to grow the economy, like education, job training, and manufacturing. The Republican proposals stand in stark contrast to the President's FY 2016 Budget, which would bring middle class economics into the 21st Century. A state-by-state breakdown of this contrast, including how the Republican budgets affect New Mexico, can be found in a report released today here: http://go.wh.gov/RoNU1j.

The President's Budget builds on the progress we've made and shows what we can do if we invest in America's future and commit to an economy that rewards hard work, generates rising incomes, and allows everyone to share in the prosperity of a growing America. It lays out a strategy to strengthen our middle class and help America's hard-working families get ahead in a time of relentless economic and technological change. And it makes the critical investments needed to accelerate and sustain economic growth in the long run, including in research, education, training, and infrastructure.

Republicans have chosen different priorities. Yet again, they are seeking to balance the budget on the backs of the middle class, while cutting taxes for the wealthy and well-connected. They still won't say where many of their spending cuts come from. But they are clear that their budgets would continue the harmful cuts known as sequestration in 2016, threatening economic growth, cutting programs middle-class families count on, and attempting to fund national security through irresponsible budget gimmicks. Their budgets slash domestic investments that support the middle-class even more significantly after 2016, along with programs that serve the most vulnerable Americans. House Republicans would end Medicare as we know it, transforming it from a guarantee seniors can count on into a voucher program. After five years of the Affordable Care Act, more than 16 million people have gained coverage. Yet once again, the Republican budgets propose to repeal the Affordable Care Act's coverage expansions.

The choice could not be more clear or the consequences more stark. Thanks to President Obama and the resilience of the American people, the economy is growing

again. The Republican budgets would put that growth at risk and limit opportunity for the middle-class and those seeking to join it.

In New Mexico, the Republican budgets would[i]:

Cut Taxes for Millionaires and Raise Taxes for Working Families and Students: While claiming to prioritize fiscal responsibility, the Republican budgets would not ask the wealthy to contribute a single dollar to deficit reduction, and the proposals specified in the House budget would cut taxes for millionaires by an average of at least $50,000. Meanwhile, the Republican budgets do nothing to prevent tax increases averaging $1,100 for 12 million families and students paying for college and $900 for 16 million working families with children. In 2015, 126,000 New Mexico families will receive a total of $118 million in tax cuts from improvements to pro-work tax credits that would expire after 2017 under the Republican budgets.

Eliminate Affordable Health Care: The Affordable Care Act is working. After five years of the Affordable Care Act, more than 16 million people have gained coverage. Yet once again, the Republican budgets propose to repeal the Affordable Care Act's coverage expansions, taking away health insurance from millions of people. In particular, the Republican budgets would eliminate coverage for 52,000 New Mexico residents who have newly signed up for coverage or re-enrolled through the Marketplaces. Some of these individuals would become uninsured while others would end up with worse or less affordable coverage.

Raise Health Care Costs for Seniors: 24,100 New Mexico seniors and people with disabilities benefited by an average of $890 from the closure of the Medicare Part D prescription drug donut hole in 2014 alone. Under the Republican plan to repeal the Affordable Care Act, at least that many would likely have to pay more for needed medications in future years. The House budget would also end Medicare as we know it, replacing guaranteed access to the traditional Medicare program with a voucher program, risking a death spiral in traditional Medicare.

Slash Investments in the Middle Class: Under the Republican budgets, both non-defense and base defense discretionary funding in 2016 would be at the lowest real levels in a decade. Compared to the President's Budget, if the Republican budgets were to take effect, these are just some of the impacts on New Mexico:

- **Head Start:** 290 fewer children in New Mexico would have access to Head Start services, representing a permanently missed opportunity to help these children enter elementary school ready to succeed.
- **Teachers and Schools:** New Mexico would receive $10.2 million less funding for disadvantaged students, an amount that is enough to fund about 50 schools, 140 teacher and aide jobs, and 20,000 students.

- **Education for Children with Disabilities:** New Mexico would receive $2.5 million less funding to provide educational opportunities for students with disabilities, representing an approximately 2.8 percent cut and shifting the burden for meeting these children's needs to New Mexico and its local communities.
- **Job Training and Employment Services:** 18,700 fewer New Mexico residents would receive job training and employment services, including help finding jobs and skills training.
- **Affordable Housing**: New Mexico would receive approximately $6.8 million less in Federal funding, resulting in 710 fewer families receiving Housing Choice Vouchers, which enable very low-income families to afford decent, safe, and sanitary housing in the private market.
- **National Parks:** Construction and renovation projects would be prevented or delayed at seven national parks in New Mexico: Capulin Volcano National Monument, Chaco Culture National Historical Park, El Morro National Monument, Pecos National Historical Park, White Sands National Monument, Bandelier National Monument, and Old Santa Fe Trail Building.

Balances Only with Gimmicks and Deep Cuts to Programs that Serve the Most Vulnerable and Help Expand Opportunity. On top of their cuts to middle-class investments and the ACA, the Republican budgets would cut:

- **Pell Grants:** Republican reductions to Pell would reduce financial aid for the 59,000 New Mexico students who rely on Pell grants to afford college.
- **Medicaid:** The House Republican proposal to block grant Medicaid would cut Federal funding to New Mexico by approximately $10.1 billion over ten years, impacting children, seniors, and people with disabilities who rely on Medicaid.
- **Supplemental Nutrition Assistance Program (SNAP):** House Republican proposals to block grant and slash SNAP would cut nutrition aid in New Mexico by an estimated $1 billion over a five year period (2021-2025), jeopardizing nutrition assistance for the 431,000 New Mexico residents who receive SNAP to help them put food on the table.

Fails to Address Our Crumbling Infrastructure: Republican budgets lack a real plan to address the looming expiration and insolvency of the Highway Trust Fund. Through the Highway Trust Fund, in FY 2014 the Federal Government obligated $361.2 million to New Mexico through the Federal Aid Highways program for highway planning and construction and over $63.3 million through Transit Formula Grants that support our Nation's mass transit systems.

i. Numbers are rounded. For a description of how impacts were calculated, see http://go.wh.gov/RoNU1j

THE WHITE HOUSE

Office of the Press Secretary

FOR IMMEDIATE RELEASE

March 24, 2015

FACT SHEET: Republican Budget Resolutions: Same Failed Top-Down Economics for New York

With more than 12 million private-sector jobs created over the last 60 months, it is clear that the President's middle class economic agenda is working. But instead of taking the steps we need to strengthen the standing of working families, the Republican budgets for fiscal year (FY) 2016 would return our economy to the same top-down economics that has failed us before: cutting taxes for millionaires and billionaires, while slashing investments in the middle class that we need to grow the economy, like education, job training, and manufacturing. The Republican proposals stand in stark contrast to the President's FY 2016 Budget, which would bring middle class economics into the 21st Century. A state-by-state breakdown of this contrast, including how the Republican budgets affect New York, can be found in a report released today here: http://go.wh.gov/RoNU1j.

The President's Budget builds on the progress we've made and shows what we can do if we invest in America's future and commit to an economy that rewards hard work, generates rising incomes, and allows everyone to share in the prosperity of a growing America. It lays out a strategy to strengthen our middle class and help America's hard-working families get ahead in a time of relentless economic and technological change. And it makes the critical investments needed to accelerate and sustain economic growth in the long run, including in research, education, training, and infrastructure.

Republicans have chosen different priorities. Yet again, they are seeking to balance the budget on the backs of the middle class, while cutting taxes for the wealthy and well-connected. They still won't say where many of their spending cuts come from. But they are clear that their budgets would continue the harmful cuts known as sequestration in 2016, threatening economic growth, cutting programs middle-class families count on, and attempting to fund national security through irresponsible budget gimmicks. Their budgets slash domestic investments that support the middle-class even more significantly after 2016, along with programs that serve the most vulnerable Americans. House Republicans would end Medicare as we know it, transforming it from a guarantee seniors can count on into a voucher program. After five years of the Affordable Care Act, more than 16 million people have gained coverage. Yet once again, the Republican budgets propose to repeal the Affordable Care Act's coverage expansions.

The choice could not be more clear or the consequences more stark. Thanks to President Obama and the resilience of the American people, the economy is growing

again. The Republican budgets would put that growth at risk and limit opportunity for the middle-class and those seeking to join it.

In New York, the Republican budgets would[i]:

Cut Taxes for Millionaires and Raise Taxes for Working Families and Students: While claiming to prioritize fiscal responsibility, the Republican budgets would not ask the wealthy to contribute a single dollar to deficit reduction, and the proposals specified in the House budget would cut taxes for millionaires by an average of at least $50,000. Meanwhile, the Republican budgets do nothing to prevent tax increases averaging $1,100 for 12 million families and students paying for college and $900 for 16 million working families with children. In 2015, 893,000 New York families will receive a total of $802 million in tax cuts from improvements to pro-work tax credits that would expire after 2017 under the Republican budgets.

Eliminate Affordable Health Care: The Affordable Care Act is working. After five years of the Affordable Care Act, more than 16 million people have gained coverage. Yet once again, the Republican budgets propose to repeal the Affordable Care Act's coverage expansions, taking away health insurance from millions of people. In particular, the Republican budgets would eliminate coverage for 409,000 New York residents who have newly signed up for coverage or re-enrolled through the Marketplaces. Some of these individuals would become uninsured while others would end up with worse or less affordable coverage.

Raise Health Care Costs for Seniors: 353,100 New York seniors and people with disabilities benefited by an average of $1,080 from the closure of the Medicare Part D prescription drug donut hole in 2014 alone. Under the Republican plan to repeal the Affordable Care Act, at least that many would likely have to pay more for needed medications in future years. The House budget would also end Medicare as we know it, replacing guaranteed access to the traditional Medicare program with a voucher program, risking a death spiral in traditional Medicare.

Slash Investments in the Middle Class: Under the Republican budgets, both non-defense and base defense discretionary funding in 2016 would be at the lowest real levels in a decade. Compared to the President's Budget, if the Republican budgets were to take effect, these are just some of the impacts on New York:

- **Head Start:** 2,330 fewer children in New York would have access to Head Start services, representing a permanently missed opportunity to help these children enter elementary school ready to succeed.
- **Teachers and Schools:** New York would receive $103.2 million less funding for disadvantaged students, an amount that is enough to fund about 300 schools, 1,420 teacher and aide jobs, and 147,000 students.

- **Education for Children with Disabilities:** New York would receive $21.2 million less funding to provide educational opportunities for students with disabilities, representing an approximately 2.8 percent cut and shifting the burden for meeting these children's needs to New York and its local communities.
- **Job Training and Employment Services:** 130,600 fewer New York residents would receive job training and employment services, including help finding jobs and skills training.
- **Affordable Housing**: New York would receive approximately $229.9 million less in Federal funding, resulting in 13,620 fewer families receiving Housing Choice Vouchers, which enable very low-income families to afford decent, safe, and sanitary housing in the private market.
- **National Parks:** Construction and renovation projects would be prevented or delayed at three national parks in New York: Fire Island National Seashore, Fort Stanwix National Monument, and Home of Franklin D. Roosevelt National Historic Site.

Balances Only with Gimmicks and Deep Cuts to Programs that Serve the Most Vulnerable and Help Expand Opportunity. On top of their cuts to middle-class investments and the ACA, the Republican budgets would cut:

- **Pell Grants:** Republican reductions to Pell would reduce financial aid for the 494,000 New York students who rely on Pell grants to afford college.
- **Medicaid:** The House Republican proposal to block grant Medicaid would cut Federal funding to New York by approximately $88.1 billion over ten years, impacting children, seniors, and people with disabilities who rely on Medicaid.
- **Supplemental Nutrition Assistance Program (SNAP):** House Republican proposals to block grant and slash SNAP would cut nutrition aid in New York by an estimated $8.2 billion over a five year period (2021-2025), jeopardizing nutrition assistance for the 3,123,000 New York residents who receive SNAP to help them put food on the table.

Fails to Address Our Crumbling Infrastructure: Republican budgets lack a real plan to address the looming expiration and insolvency of the Highway Trust Fund. Through the Highway Trust Fund, in FY 2014 the Federal Government obligated $1.9 billion to New York through the Federal Aid Highways program for highway planning and construction and over $1.8 billion through Transit Formula Grants that support our Nation's mass transit systems.

i. Numbers are rounded. For a description of how impacts were calculated, see http://go.wh.gov/RoNU1j

FOR IMMEDIATE RELEASE
March 24, 2015

FACT SHEET: Republican Budget Resolutions: Same Failed Top-Down Economics for North Carolina

With more than 12 million private-sector jobs created over the last 60 months, it is clear that the President's middle class economic agenda is working. But instead of taking the steps we need to strengthen the standing of working families, the Republican budgets for fiscal year (FY) 2016 would return our economy to the same top-down economics that has failed us before: cutting taxes for millionaires and billionaires, while slashing investments in the middle class that we need to grow the economy, like education, job training, and manufacturing. The Republican proposals stand in stark contrast to the President's FY 2016 Budget, which would bring middle class economics into the 21st Century. A state-by-state breakdown of this contrast, including how the Republican budgets affect North Carolina, can be found in a report released today here: http://go.wh.gov/RoNU1j.

The President's Budget builds on the progress we've made and shows what we can do if we invest in America's future and commit to an economy that rewards hard work, generates rising incomes, and allows everyone to share in the prosperity of a growing America. It lays out a strategy to strengthen our middle class and help America's hard-working families get ahead in a time of relentless economic and technological change. And it makes the critical investments needed to accelerate and sustain economic growth in the long run, including in research, education, training, and infrastructure.

Republicans have chosen different priorities. Yet again, they are seeking to balance the budget on the backs of the middle class, while cutting taxes for the wealthy and well-connected. They still won't say where many of their spending cuts come from. But they are clear that their budgets would continue the harmful cuts known as sequestration in 2016, threatening economic growth, cutting programs middle-class families count on, and attempting to fund national security through irresponsible budget gimmicks. Their budgets slash domestic investments that support the middle-class even more significantly after 2016, along with programs that serve the most vulnerable Americans. House Republicans would end Medicare as we know it, transforming it from a guarantee seniors can count on into a voucher program. After five years of the Affordable Care Act, more than 16 million people have gained coverage. Yet once again, the Republican budgets propose to repeal the Affordable Care Act's coverage expansions.

The choice could not be more clear or the consequences more stark. Thanks to President Obama and the resilience of the American people, the economy is growing

again. The Republican budgets would put that growth at risk and limit opportunity for the middle-class and those seeking to join it.

In North Carolina, the Republican budgets would[i]:

Cut Taxes for Millionaires and Raise Taxes for Working Families and Students:
While claiming to prioritize fiscal responsibility, the Republican budgets would not ask the wealthy to contribute a single dollar to deficit reduction, and the proposals specified in the House budget would cut taxes for millionaires by an average of at least $50,000. Meanwhile, the Republican budgets do nothing to prevent tax increases averaging $1,100 for 12 million families and students paying for college and $900 for 16 million working families with children. In 2015, 552,000 North Carolina families will receive a total of $498 million in tax cuts from improvements to pro-work tax credits that would expire after 2017 under the Republican budgets.

Eliminate Affordable Health Care: The Affordable Care Act is working. After five years of the Affordable Care Act, more than 16 million people have gained coverage. Yet once again, the Republican budgets propose to repeal the Affordable Care Act's coverage expansions, taking away health insurance from millions of people. In particular, the Republican budgets would eliminate coverage for 560,000 North Carolina residents who have newly signed up for coverage or re-enrolled through the Marketplaces. Some of these individuals would become uninsured while others would end up with worse or less affordable coverage.

Raise Health Care Costs for Seniors: 174,500 North Carolina seniors and people with disabilities benefited by an average of $880 from the closure of the Medicare Part D prescription drug donut hole in 2014 alone. Under the Republican plan to repeal the Affordable Care Act, at least that many would likely have to pay more for needed medications in future years. The House budget would also end Medicare as we know it, replacing guaranteed access to the traditional Medicare program with a voucher program, risking a death spiral in traditional Medicare.

Slash Investments in the Middle Class: Under the Republican budgets, both non-defense and base defense discretionary funding in 2016 would be at the lowest real levels in a decade. Compared to the President's Budget, if the Republican budgets were to take effect, these are just some of the impacts on North Carolina:

- **Head Start:** 790 fewer children in North Carolina would have access to Head Start services, representing a permanently missed opportunity to help these children enter elementary school ready to succeed.
- **Teachers and Schools:** North Carolina would receive $36.7 million less funding for disadvantaged students, an amount that is enough to fund about 110 schools, 500 teacher and aide jobs, and 54,000 students.

- **Education for Children with Disabilities:** North Carolina would receive $9.7 million less funding to provide educational opportunities for students with disabilities, representing an approximately 2.9 percent cut and shifting the burden for meeting these children's needs to North Carolina and its local communities.
- **Job Training and Employment Services:** 65,900 fewer North Carolina residents would receive job training and employment services, including help finding jobs and skills training.
- **Affordable Housing:** North Carolina would receive approximately $32.9 million less in Federal funding, resulting in 3,320 fewer families receiving Housing Choice Vouchers, which enable very low-income families to afford decent, safe, and sanitary housing in the private market.
- **National Parks:** Construction and renovation projects would be prevented or delayed at six national parks in North Carolina: Blue Ridge Parkway, Carl Sandburg Home National Historic Site, Moores Creek National Battlefield, Appalachian National Scenic Trail, Cape Hatteras National Seashore, and Guilford Courthouse National Military Park.

Balances Only with Gimmicks and Deep Cuts to Programs that Serve the Most Vulnerable and Help Expand Opportunity. On top of their cuts to middle-class investments and the ACA, the Republican budgets would cut:

- **Pell Grants:** Republican reductions to Pell would reduce financial aid for the 215,000 North Carolina students who rely on Pell grants to afford college.
- **Medicaid:** The House Republican proposal to block grant Medicaid would cut Federal funding to North Carolina by approximately $26.0 billion over ten years, impacting children, seniors, and people with disabilities who rely on Medicaid.
- **Supplemental Nutrition Assistance Program (SNAP):** House Republican proposals to block grant and slash SNAP would cut nutrition aid in North Carolina by an estimated $3.8 billion over a five year period (2021-2025), jeopardizing nutrition assistance for the 1,576,000 North Carolina residents who receive SNAP to help them put food on the table.

Fails to Address Our Crumbling Infrastructure: Republican budgets lack a real plan to address the looming expiration and insolvency of the Highway Trust Fund. Through the Highway Trust Fund, in FY 2014 the Federal Government obligated $969.2 million to North Carolina through the Federal Aid Highways program for highway planning and construction and over $156.1 million through Transit Formula Grants that support our Nation's mass transit systems.

i. Numbers are rounded. For a description of how impacts were calculated, see http://go.wh.gov/RoNU1j

THE WHITE HOUSE
Office of the Press Secretary

FOR IMMEDIATE RELEASE
March 24, 2015

FACT SHEET: Republican Budget Resolutions: Same Failed Top-Down Economics for North Dakota

With more than 12 million private-sector jobs created over the last 60 months, it is clear that the President's middle class economic agenda is working. But instead of taking the steps we need to strengthen the standing of working families, the Republican budgets for fiscal year (FY) 2016 would return our economy to the same top-down economics that has failed us before: cutting taxes for millionaires and billionaires, while slashing investments in the middle class that we need to grow the economy, like education, job training, and manufacturing. The Republican proposals stand in stark contrast to the President's FY 2016 Budget, which would bring middle class economics into the 21st Century. A state-by-state breakdown of this contrast, including how the Republican budgets affect North Dakota, can be found in a report released today here: http://go.wh.gov/RoNU1j.

The President's Budget builds on the progress we've made and shows what we can do if we invest in America's future and commit to an economy that rewards hard work, generates rising incomes, and allows everyone to share in the prosperity of a growing America. It lays out a strategy to strengthen our middle class and help America's hard-working families get ahead in a time of relentless economic and technological change. And it makes the critical investments needed to accelerate and sustain economic growth in the long run, including in research, education, training, and infrastructure.

Republicans have chosen different priorities. Yet again, they are seeking to balance the budget on the backs of the middle class, while cutting taxes for the wealthy and well-connected. They still won't say where many of their spending cuts come from. But they are clear that their budgets would continue the harmful cuts known as sequestration in 2016, threatening economic growth, cutting programs middle-class families count on, and attempting to fund national security through irresponsible budget gimmicks. Their budgets slash domestic investments that support the middle-class even more significantly after 2016, along with programs that serve the most vulnerable Americans. House Republicans would end Medicare as we know it, transforming it from a guarantee seniors can count on into a voucher program. After five years of the Affordable Care Act, more than 16 million people have gained coverage. Yet once again, the Republican budgets propose to repeal the Affordable Care Act's coverage expansions.

The choice could not be more clear or the consequences more stark. Thanks to President Obama and the resilience of the American people, the economy is growing

again. The Republican budgets would put that growth at risk and limit opportunity for the middle-class and those seeking to join it.

In North Dakota, the Republican budgets would[i]:

Cut Taxes for Millionaires and Raise Taxes for Working Families and Students: While claiming to prioritize fiscal responsibility, the Republican budgets would not ask the wealthy to contribute a single dollar to deficit reduction, and the proposals specified in the House budget would cut taxes for millionaires by an average of at least $50,000. Meanwhile, the Republican budgets do nothing to prevent tax increases averaging $1,100 for 12 million families and students paying for college and $900 for 16 million working families with children. In 2015, 24,000 North Dakota families will receive a total of $20 million in tax cuts from improvements to pro-work tax credits that would expire after 2017 under the Republican budgets.

Eliminate Affordable Health Care: The Affordable Care Act is working. After five years of the Affordable Care Act, more than 16 million people have gained coverage. Yet once again, the Republican budgets propose to repeal the Affordable Care Act's coverage expansions, taking away health insurance from millions of people. In particular, the Republican budgets would eliminate coverage for 18,000 North Dakota residents who have newly signed up for coverage or re-enrolled through the Marketplaces. Some of these individuals would become uninsured while others would end up with worse or less affordable coverage.

Raise Health Care Costs for Seniors: 11,300 North Dakota seniors and people with disabilities benefited by an average of $850 from the closure of the Medicare Part D prescription drug donut hole in 2014 alone. Under the Republican plan to repeal the Affordable Care Act, at least that many would likely have to pay more for needed medications in future years. The House budget would also end Medicare as we know it, replacing guaranteed access to the traditional Medicare program with a voucher program, risking a death spiral in traditional Medicare.

Slash Investments in the Middle Class: Under the Republican budgets, both non-defense and base defense discretionary funding in 2016 would be at the lowest real levels in a decade. Compared to the President's Budget, if the Republican budgets were to take effect, these are just some of the impacts on North Dakota:

- **Head Start:** 90 fewer children in North Dakota would have access to Head Start services, representing a permanently missed opportunity to help these children enter elementary school ready to succeed.
- **Teachers and Schools:** North Dakota would receive $3.2 million less funding for disadvantaged students, an amount that is enough to fund about 20 schools, 40 teacher and aide jobs, and 3,000 students.

- **Education for Children with Disabilities:** North Dakota would receive $1.3 million less funding to provide educational opportunities for students with disabilities, representing an approximately 4.5 percent cut and shifting the burden for meeting these children's needs to North Dakota and its local communities.
- **Job Training and Employment Services:** 17,000 fewer North Dakota residents would receive job training and employment services, including help finding jobs and skills training.
- **Affordable Housing**: North Dakota would receive approximately $3.0 million less in Federal funding, resulting in 390 fewer families receiving Housing Choice Vouchers, which enable very low-income families to afford decent, safe, and sanitary housing in the private market.

Balances Only with Gimmicks and Deep Cuts to Programs that Serve the Most Vulnerable and Help Expand Opportunity. On top of their cuts to middle-class investments and the ACA, the Republican budgets would cut:

- **Pell Grants:** Republican reductions to Pell would reduce financial aid for the 13,000 North Dakota students who rely on Pell grants to afford college.
- **Medicaid:** The House Republican proposal to block grant Medicaid would cut Federal funding to North Dakota by approximately $0.7 billion over ten years, impacting children, seniors, and people with disabilities who rely on Medicaid.
- **Supplemental Nutrition Assistance Program (SNAP):** House Republican proposals to block grant and slash SNAP would cut nutrition aid in North Dakota by an estimated $100 million over a five year period (2021-2025), jeopardizing nutrition assistance for the 54,000 North Dakota residents who receive SNAP to help them put food on the table.

Fails to Address Our Crumbling Infrastructure: Republican budgets lack a real plan to address the looming expiration and insolvency of the Highway Trust Fund. Through the Highway Trust Fund, in FY 2014 the Federal Government obligated $260.9 million to North Dakota through the Federal Aid Highways program for highway planning and construction and over $18.5 million through Transit Formula Grants that support our Nation's mass transit systems.

i. Numbers are rounded. For a description of how impacts were calculated, see http://go.wh.gov/RoNU1j

THE WHITE HOUSE
Office of the Press Secretary

FOR IMMEDIATE RELEASE
March 24, 2015

FACT SHEET: Republican Budget Resolutions: Same Failed Top-Down Economics for Ohio

With more than 12 million private-sector jobs created over the last 60 months, it is clear that the President's middle class economic agenda is working. But instead of taking the steps we need to strengthen the standing of working families, the Republican budgets for fiscal year (FY) 2016 would return our economy to the same top-down economics that has failed us before: cutting taxes for millionaires and billionaires, while slashing investments in the middle class that we need to grow the economy, like education, job training, and manufacturing. The Republican proposals stand in stark contrast to the President's FY 2016 Budget, which would bring middle class economics into the 21st Century. A state-by-state breakdown of this contrast, including how the Republican budgets affect Ohio, can be found in a report released today here: http://go.wh.gov/RoNU1j.

The President's Budget builds on the progress we've made and shows what we can do if we invest in America's future and commit to an economy that rewards hard work, generates rising incomes, and allows everyone to share in the prosperity of a growing America. It lays out a strategy to strengthen our middle class and help America's hard-working families get ahead in a time of relentless economic and technological change. And it makes the critical investments needed to accelerate and sustain economic growth in the long run, including in research, education, training, and infrastructure.

Republicans have chosen different priorities. Yet again, they are seeking to balance the budget on the backs of the middle class, while cutting taxes for the wealthy and well-connected. They still won't say where many of their spending cuts come from. But they are clear that their budgets would continue the harmful cuts known as sequestration in 2016, threatening economic growth, cutting programs middle-class families count on, and attempting to fund national security through irresponsible budget gimmicks. Their budgets slash domestic investments that support the middle-class even more significantly after 2016, along with programs that serve the most vulnerable Americans. House Republicans would end Medicare as we know it, transforming it from a guarantee seniors can count on into a voucher program. After five years of the Affordable Care Act, more than 16 million people have gained coverage. Yet once again, the Republican budgets propose to repeal the Affordable Care Act's coverage expansions.

The choice could not be more clear or the consequences more stark. Thanks to President Obama and the resilience of the American people, the economy is growing

again. The Republican budgets would put that growth at risk and limit opportunity for the middle-class and those seeking to join it.

In Ohio, the Republican budgets would[i]:

Cut Taxes for Millionaires and Raise Taxes for Working Families and Students: While claiming to prioritize fiscal responsibility, the Republican budgets would not ask the wealthy to contribute a single dollar to deficit reduction, and the proposals specified in the House budget would cut taxes for millionaires by an average of at least $50,000. Meanwhile, the Republican budgets do nothing to prevent tax increases averaging $1,100 for 12 million families and students paying for college and $900 for 16 million working families with children. In 2015, 546,000 Ohio families will receive a total of $490 million in tax cuts from improvements to pro-work tax credits that would expire after 2017 under the Republican budgets.

Eliminate Affordable Health Care: The Affordable Care Act is working. After five years of the Affordable Care Act, more than 16 million people have gained coverage. Yet once again, the Republican budgets propose to repeal the Affordable Care Act's coverage expansions, taking away health insurance from millions of people. In particular, the Republican budgets would eliminate coverage for 234,000 Ohio residents who have newly signed up for coverage or re-enrolled through the Marketplaces. Some of these individuals would become uninsured while others would end up with worse or less affordable coverage.

Raise Health Care Costs for Seniors: 239,700 Ohio seniors and people with disabilities benefited by an average of $980 from the closure of the Medicare Part D prescription drug donut hole in 2014 alone. Under the Republican plan to repeal the Affordable Care Act, at least that many would likely have to pay more for needed medications in future years. The House budget would also end Medicare as we know it, replacing guaranteed access to the traditional Medicare program with a voucher program, risking a death spiral in traditional Medicare.

Slash Investments in the Middle Class: Under the Republican budgets, both non-defense and base defense discretionary funding in 2016 would be at the lowest real levels in a decade. Compared to the President's Budget, if the Republican budgets were to take effect, these are just some of the impacts on Ohio:

- **Head Start:** 1,340 fewer children in Ohio would have access to Head Start services, representing a permanently missed opportunity to help these children enter elementary school ready to succeed.
- **Teachers and Schools:** Ohio would receive $44.5 million less funding for disadvantaged students, an amount that is enough to fund about 180 schools, 610 teacher and aide jobs, and 60,000 students.

- **Education for Children with Disabilities:** Ohio would receive $12.5 million less funding to provide educational opportunities for students with disabilities, representing an approximately 2.9 percent cut and shifting the burden for meeting these children's needs to Ohio and its local communities.
- **Job Training and Employment Services:** 79,800 fewer Ohio residents would receive job training and employment services, including help finding jobs and skills training.
- **Affordable Housing**: Ohio would receive approximately $52.4 million less in Federal funding, resulting in 5,660 fewer families receiving Housing Choice Vouchers, which enable very low-income families to afford decent, safe, and sanitary housing in the private market.

Balances Only with Gimmicks and Deep Cuts to Programs that Serve the Most Vulnerable and Help Expand Opportunity. On top of their cuts to middle-class investments and the ACA, the Republican budgets would cut:

- **Pell Grants:** Republican reductions to Pell would reduce financial aid for the 260,000 Ohio students who rely on Pell grants to afford college.
- **Medicaid:** The House Republican proposal to block grant Medicaid would cut Federal funding to Ohio by approximately $42.0 billion over ten years, impacting children, seniors, and people with disabilities who rely on Medicaid.
- **Supplemental Nutrition Assistance Program (SNAP):** House Republican proposals to block grant and slash SNAP would cut nutrition aid in Ohio by an estimated $4.1 billion over a five year period (2021-2025), jeopardizing nutrition assistance for the 1,752,000 Ohio residents who receive SNAP to help them put food on the table.

Fails to Address Our Crumbling Infrastructure: Republican budgets lack a real plan to address the looming expiration and insolvency of the Highway Trust Fund. Through the Highway Trust Fund, in FY 2014 the Federal Government obligated $1.3 billion to Ohio through the Federal Aid Highways program for highway planning and construction and over $286.4 million through Transit Formula Grants that support our Nation's mass transit systems.

i. Numbers are rounded. For a description of how impacts were calculated, see http://go.wh.gov/RoNU1j

FOR IMMEDIATE RELEASE
March 24, 2015

FACT SHEET: Republican Budget Resolutions: Same Failed Top-Down Economics for Oklahoma

With more than 12 million private-sector jobs created over the last 60 months, it is clear that the President's middle class economic agenda is working. But instead of taking the steps we need to strengthen the standing of working families, the Republican budgets for fiscal year (FY) 2016 would return our economy to the same top-down economics that has failed us before: cutting taxes for millionaires and billionaires, while slashing investments in the middle class that we need to grow the economy, like education, job training, and manufacturing. The Republican proposals stand in stark contrast to the President's FY 2016 Budget, which would bring middle class economics into the 21st Century. A state-by-state breakdown of this contrast, including how the Republican budgets affect Oklahoma, can be found in a report released today here: http://go.wh.gov/RoNU1j.

The President's Budget builds on the progress we've made and shows what we can do if we invest in America's future and commit to an economy that rewards hard work, generates rising incomes, and allows everyone to share in the prosperity of a growing America. It lays out a strategy to strengthen our middle class and help America's hard-working families get ahead in a time of relentless economic and technological change. And it makes the critical investments needed to accelerate and sustain economic growth in the long run, including in research, education, training, and infrastructure.

Republicans have chosen different priorities. Yet again, they are seeking to balance the budget on the backs of the middle class, while cutting taxes for the wealthy and well-connected. They still won't say where many of their spending cuts come from. But they are clear that their budgets would continue the harmful cuts known as sequestration in 2016, threatening economic growth, cutting programs middle-class families count on, and attempting to fund national security through irresponsible budget gimmicks. Their budgets slash domestic investments that support the middle-class even more significantly after 2016, along with programs that serve the most vulnerable Americans. House Republicans would end Medicare as we know it, transforming it from a guarantee seniors can count on into a voucher program. After five years of the Affordable Care Act, more than 16 million people have gained coverage. Yet once again, the Republican budgets propose to repeal the Affordable Care Act's coverage expansions.

The choice could not be more clear or the consequences more stark. Thanks to President Obama and the resilience of the American people, the economy is growing

again. The Republican budgets would put that growth at risk and limit opportunity for the middle-class and those seeking to join it.

In Oklahoma, the Republican budgets would[i]:

Cut Taxes for Millionaires and Raise Taxes for Working Families and Students: While claiming to prioritize fiscal responsibility, the Republican budgets would not ask the wealthy to contribute a single dollar to deficit reduction, and the proposals specified in the House budget would cut taxes for millionaires by an average of at least $50,000. Meanwhile, the Republican budgets do nothing to prevent tax increases averaging $1,100 for 12 million families and students paying for college and $900 for 16 million working families with children. In 2015, 212,000 Oklahoma families will receive a total of $193 million in tax cuts from improvements to pro-work tax credits that would expire after 2017 under the Republican budgets.

Eliminate Affordable Health Care: The Affordable Care Act is working. After five years of the Affordable Care Act, more than 16 million people have gained coverage. Yet once again, the Republican budgets propose to repeal the Affordable Care Act's coverage expansions, taking away health insurance from millions of people. In particular, the Republican budgets would eliminate coverage for 126,000 Oklahoma residents who have newly signed up for coverage or re-enrolled through the Marketplaces. Some of these individuals would become uninsured while others would end up with worse or less affordable coverage.

Raise Health Care Costs for Seniors: 65,200 Oklahoma seniors and people with disabilities benefited by an average of $930 from the closure of the Medicare Part D prescription drug donut hole in 2014 alone. Under the Republican plan to repeal the Affordable Care Act, at least that many would likely have to pay more for needed medications in future years. The House budget would also end Medicare as we know it, replacing guaranteed access to the traditional Medicare program with a voucher program, risking a death spiral in traditional Medicare.

Slash Investments in the Middle Class: Under the Republican budgets, both non-defense and base defense discretionary funding in 2016 would be at the lowest real levels in a decade. Compared to the President's Budget, if the Republican budgets were to take effect, these are just some of the impacts on Oklahoma:

- **Head Start:** 460 fewer children in Oklahoma would have access to Head Start services, representing a permanently missed opportunity to help these children enter elementary school ready to succeed.
- **Teachers and Schools:** Oklahoma would receive $12.8 million less funding for disadvantaged students, an amount that is enough to fund about 100 schools, 180 teacher and aide jobs, and 33,000 students.

- **Education for Children with Disabilities:** Oklahoma would receive $4.2 million less funding to provide educational opportunities for students with disabilities, representing an approximately 2.8 percent cut and shifting the burden for meeting these children's needs to Oklahoma and its local communities.
- **Job Training and Employment Services:** 22,000 fewer Oklahoma residents would receive job training and employment services, including help finding jobs and skills training.
- **Affordable Housing**: Oklahoma would receive approximately $12.1 million less in Federal funding, resulting in 1,400 fewer families receiving Housing Choice Vouchers, which enable very low-income families to afford decent, safe, and sanitary housing in the private market.
- **National Parks:** Construction and renovation projects would be prevented or delayed at Chickasaw National Recreation Area.

Balances Only with Gimmicks and Deep Cuts to Programs that Serve the Most Vulnerable and Help Expand Opportunity. On top of their cuts to middle-class investments and the ACA, the Republican budgets would cut:

- **Pell Grants:** Republican reductions to Pell would reduce financial aid for the 91,000 Oklahoma students who rely on Pell grants to afford college.
- **Medicaid:** The House Republican proposal to block grant Medicaid would cut Federal funding to Oklahoma by approximately $10.0 billion over ten years, impacting children, seniors, and people with disabilities who rely on Medicaid.
- **Supplemental Nutrition Assistance Program (SNAP):** House Republican proposals to block grant and slash SNAP would cut nutrition aid in Oklahoma by an estimated $1.4 billion over a five year period (2021-2025), jeopardizing nutrition assistance for the 608,000 Oklahoma residents who receive SNAP to help them put food on the table.

Fails to Address Our Crumbling Infrastructure: Republican budgets lack a real plan to address the looming expiration and insolvency of the Highway Trust Fund. Through the Highway Trust Fund, in FY 2014 the Federal Government obligated $625.3 million to Oklahoma through the Federal Aid Highways program for highway planning and construction and over $28.5 million through Transit Formula Grants that support our Nation's mass transit systems.

i. Numbers are rounded. For a description of how impacts were calculated, see http://go.wh.gov/RoNU1j

FOR IMMEDIATE RELEASE
March 24, 2015

FACT SHEET: Republican Budget Resolutions: Same Failed Top-Down Economics for Oregon

With more than 12 million private-sector jobs created over the last 60 months, it is clear that the President's middle class economic agenda is working. But instead of taking the steps we need to strengthen the standing of working families, the Republican budgets for fiscal year (FY) 2016 would return our economy to the same top-down economics that has failed us before: cutting taxes for millionaires and billionaires, while slashing investments in the middle class that we need to grow the economy, like education, job training, and manufacturing. The Republican proposals stand in stark contrast to the President's FY 2016 Budget, which would bring middle class economics into the 21st Century. A state-by-state breakdown of this contrast, including how the Republican budgets affect Oregon, can be found in a report released today here: http://go.wh.gov/RoNU1j.

The President's Budget builds on the progress we've made and shows what we can do if we invest in America's future and commit to an economy that rewards hard work, generates rising incomes, and allows everyone to share in the prosperity of a growing America. It lays out a strategy to strengthen our middle class and help America's hard-working families get ahead in a time of relentless economic and technological change. And it makes the critical investments needed to accelerate and sustain economic growth in the long run, including in research, education, training, and infrastructure.

Republicans have chosen different priorities. Yet again, they are seeking to balance the budget on the backs of the middle class, while cutting taxes for the wealthy and well-connected. They still won't say where many of their spending cuts come from. But they are clear that their budgets would continue the harmful cuts known as sequestration in 2016, threatening economic growth, cutting programs middle-class families count on, and attempting to fund national security through irresponsible budget gimmicks. Their budgets slash domestic investments that support the middle-class even more significantly after 2016, along with programs that serve the most vulnerable Americans. House Republicans would end Medicare as we know it, transforming it from a guarantee seniors can count on into a voucher program. After five years of the Affordable Care Act, more than 16 million people have gained coverage. Yet once again, the Republican budgets propose to repeal the Affordable Care Act's coverage expansions.

The choice could not be more clear or the consequences more stark. Thanks to President Obama and the resilience of the American people, the economy is growing

again. The Republican budgets would put that growth at risk and limit opportunity for the middle-class and those seeking to join it.

In Oregon, the Republican budgets would[i]:

Cut Taxes for Millionaires and Raise Taxes for Working Families and Students:
While claiming to prioritize fiscal responsibility, the Republican budgets would not ask the wealthy to contribute a single dollar to deficit reduction, and the proposals specified in the House budget would cut taxes for millionaires by an average of at least $50,000. Meanwhile, the Republican budgets do nothing to prevent tax increases averaging $1,100 for 12 million families and students paying for college and $900 for 16 million working families with children. In 2015, 173,000 Oregon families will receive a total of $156 million in tax cuts from improvements to pro-work tax credits that would expire after 2017 under the Republican budgets.

Eliminate Affordable Health Care: The Affordable Care Act is working. After five years of the Affordable Care Act, more than 16 million people have gained coverage. Yet once again, the Republican budgets propose to repeal the Affordable Care Act's coverage expansions, taking away health insurance from millions of people. In particular, the Republican budgets would eliminate coverage for 112,000 Oregon residents who have newly signed up for coverage or re-enrolled through the Marketplaces. Some of these individuals would become uninsured while others would end up with worse or less affordable coverage.

Raise Health Care Costs for Seniors: 52,600 Oregon seniors and people with disabilities benefited by an average of $810 from the closure of the Medicare Part D prescription drug donut hole in 2014 alone. Under the Republican plan to repeal the Affordable Care Act, at least that many would likely have to pay more for needed medications in future years. The House budget would also end Medicare as we know it, replacing guaranteed access to the traditional Medicare program with a voucher program, risking a death spiral in traditional Medicare.

Slash Investments in the Middle Class: Under the Republican budgets, both non-defense and base defense discretionary funding in 2016 would be at the lowest real levels in a decade. Compared to the President's Budget, if the Republican budgets were to take effect, these are just some of the impacts on Oregon:

- **Head Start:** 330 fewer children in Oregon would have access to Head Start services, representing a permanently missed opportunity to help these children enter elementary school ready to succeed.
- **Teachers and Schools:** Oregon would receive $11.3 million less funding for disadvantaged students, an amount that is enough to fund about 40 schools, 160 teacher and aide jobs, and 15,000 students.

- **Education for Children with Disabilities:** Oregon would receive $3.7 million less funding to provide educational opportunities for students with disabilities, representing an approximately 2.8 percent cut and shifting the burden for meeting these children's needs to Oregon and its local communities.
- **Job Training and Employment Services:** 27,500 fewer Oregon residents would receive job training and employment services, including help finding jobs and skills training.
- **Affordable Housing:** Oregon would receive approximately $20.9 million less in Federal funding, resulting in 2,050 fewer families receiving Housing Choice Vouchers, which enable very low-income families to afford decent, safe, and sanitary housing in the private market.

Balances Only with Gimmicks and Deep Cuts to Programs that Serve the Most Vulnerable and Help Expand Opportunity. On top of their cuts to middle-class investments and the ACA, the Republican budgets would cut:

- **Pell Grants:** Republican reductions to Pell would reduce financial aid for the 114,000 Oregon students who rely on Pell grants to afford college.
- **Medicaid:** The House Republican proposal to block grant Medicaid would cut Federal funding to Oregon by approximately $16.2 billion over ten years, impacting children, seniors, and people with disabilities who rely on Medicaid.
- **Supplemental Nutrition Assistance Program (SNAP):** House Republican proposals to block grant and slash SNAP would cut nutrition aid in Oregon by an estimated $1.8 billion over a five year period (2021-2025), jeopardizing nutrition assistance for the 802,000 Oregon residents who receive SNAP to help them put food on the table.

Fails to Address Our Crumbling Infrastructure: Republican budgets lack a real plan to address the looming expiration and insolvency of the Highway Trust Fund. Through the Highway Trust Fund, in FY 2014 the Federal Government obligated $461.6 million to Oregon through the Federal Aid Highways program for highway planning and construction and over $214.8 million through Transit Formula Grants that support our Nation's mass transit systems.

i. Numbers are rounded. For a description of how impacts were calculated, see http://go.wh.gov/RoNU1j

FOR IMMEDIATE RELEASE
March 24, 2015

FACT SHEET: Republican Budget Resolutions: Same Failed Top-Down Economics for Pennsylvania

With more than 12 million private-sector jobs created over the last 60 months, it is clear that the President's middle class economic agenda is working. But instead of taking the steps we need to strengthen the standing of working families, the Republican budgets for fiscal year (FY) 2016 would return our economy to the same top-down economics that has failed us before: cutting taxes for millionaires and billionaires, while slashing investments in the middle class that we need to grow the economy, like education, job training, and manufacturing. The Republican proposals stand in stark contrast to the President's FY 2016 Budget, which would bring middle class economics into the 21st Century. A state-by-state breakdown of this contrast, including how the Republican budgets affect Pennsylvania, can be found in a report released today here: http://go.wh.gov/RoNU1j.

The President's Budget builds on the progress we've made and shows what we can do if we invest in America's future and commit to an economy that rewards hard work, generates rising incomes, and allows everyone to share in the prosperity of a growing America. It lays out a strategy to strengthen our middle class and help America's hard-working families get ahead in a time of relentless economic and technological change. And it makes the critical investments needed to accelerate and sustain economic growth in the long run, including in research, education, training, and infrastructure.

Republicans have chosen different priorities. Yet again, they are seeking to balance the budget on the backs of the middle class, while cutting taxes for the wealthy and well-connected. They still won't say where many of their spending cuts come from. But they are clear that their budgets would continue the harmful cuts known as sequestration in 2016, threatening economic growth, cutting programs middle-class families count on, and attempting to fund national security through irresponsible budget gimmicks. Their budgets slash domestic investments that support the middle-class even more significantly after 2016, along with programs that serve the most vulnerable Americans. House Republicans would end Medicare as we know it, transforming it from a guarantee seniors can count on into a voucher program. After five years of the Affordable Care Act, more than 16 million people have gained coverage. Yet once again, the Republican budgets propose to repeal the Affordable Care Act's coverage expansions.

The choice could not be more clear or the consequences more stark. Thanks to President Obama and the resilience of the American people, the economy is growing

again. The Republican budgets would put that growth at risk and limit opportunity for the middle-class and those seeking to join it.

In Pennsylvania, the Republican budgets would[i]:

Cut Taxes for Millionaires and Raise Taxes for Working Families and Students: While claiming to prioritize fiscal responsibility, the Republican budgets would not ask the wealthy to contribute a single dollar to deficit reduction, and the proposals specified in the House budget would cut taxes for millionaires by an average of at least $50,000. Meanwhile, the Republican budgets do nothing to prevent tax increases averaging $1,100 for 12 million families and students paying for college and $900 for 16 million working families with children. In 2015, 486,000 Pennsylvania families will receive a total of $423 million in tax cuts from improvements to pro-work tax credits that would expire after 2017 under the Republican budgets.

Eliminate Affordable Health Care: The Affordable Care Act is working. After five years of the Affordable Care Act, more than 16 million people have gained coverage. Yet once again, the Republican budgets propose to repeal the Affordable Care Act's coverage expansions, taking away health insurance from millions of people. In particular, the Republican budgets would eliminate coverage for 473,000 Pennsylvania residents who have newly signed up for coverage or re-enrolled through the Marketplaces. Some of these individuals would become uninsured while others would end up with worse or less affordable coverage.

Raise Health Care Costs for Seniors: 297,100 Pennsylvania seniors and people with disabilities benefited by an average of $950 from the closure of the Medicare Part D prescription drug donut hole in 2014 alone. Under the Republican plan to repeal the Affordable Care Act, at least that many would likely have to pay more for needed medications in future years. The House budget would also end Medicare as we know it, replacing guaranteed access to the traditional Medicare program with a voucher program, risking a death spiral in traditional Medicare.

Slash Investments in the Middle Class: Under the Republican budgets, both non-defense and base defense discretionary funding in 2016 would be at the lowest real levels in a decade. Compared to the President's Budget, if the Republican budgets were to take effect, these are just some of the impacts on Pennsylvania:

- **Head Start:** 1,250 fewer children in Pennsylvania would have access to Head Start services, representing a permanently missed opportunity to help these children enter elementary school ready to succeed.
- **Teachers and Schools:** Pennsylvania would receive $44.1 million less funding for disadvantaged students, an amount that is enough to fund about 140 schools, 610 teacher and aide jobs, and 49,000 students.

- **Education for Children with Disabilities:** Pennsylvania would receive $12.2 million less funding to provide educational opportunities for students with disabilities, representing an approximately 2.8 percent cut and shifting the burden for meeting these children's needs to Pennsylvania and its local communities.
- **Job Training and Employment Services:** 87,000 fewer Pennsylvania residents would receive job training and employment services, including help finding jobs and skills training.
- **Affordable Housing**: Pennsylvania would receive approximately $55.8 million less in Federal funding, resulting in 4,620 fewer families receiving Housing Choice Vouchers, which enable very low-income families to afford decent, safe, and sanitary housing in the private market.
- **National Parks:** Construction and renovation projects would be prevented or delayed at seven national parks in Pennsylvania: Allegheny Portage Railroad National Historic Site, Delaware Water Gap National Recreation Area, Eisenhower National Historic Site, Fort Necessity National Battlefield, Johnstown Flood National Memorial, Valley Forge National Historical Park, and Appalachian National Scenic Trail.

Balances Only with Gimmicks and Deep Cuts to Programs that Serve the Most Vulnerable and Help Expand Opportunity. On top of their cuts to middle-class investments and the ACA, the Republican budgets would cut:

- **Pell Grants:** Republican reductions to Pell would reduce financial aid for the 262,000 Pennsylvania students who rely on Pell grants to afford college.
- **Medicaid:** The House Republican proposal to block grant Medicaid would cut Federal funding to Pennsylvania by approximately $41.2 billion over ten years, impacting children, seniors, and people with disabilities who rely on Medicaid.
- **Supplemental Nutrition Assistance Program (SNAP):** House Republican proposals to block grant and slash SNAP would cut nutrition aid in Pennsylvania by an estimated $4.1 billion over a five year period (2021-2025), jeopardizing nutrition assistance for the 1,796,000 Pennsylvania residents who receive SNAP to help them put food on the table.

Fails to Address Our Crumbling Infrastructure: Republican budgets lack a real plan to address the looming expiration and insolvency of the Highway Trust Fund. Through the Highway Trust Fund, in FY 2014 the Federal Government obligated $1.6 billion to Pennsylvania through the Federal Aid Highways program for highway planning and construction and over $615.1 million through Transit Formula Grants that support our Nation's mass transit systems.

###

i. Numbers are rounded. For a description of how impacts were calculated, see http://go.wh.gov/RoNUIj

FOR IMMEDIATE RELEASE
March 24, 2015

FACT SHEET: Republican Budget Resolutions: Same Failed Top-Down Economics for Rhode Island

With more than 12 million private-sector jobs created over the last 60 months, it is clear that the President's middle class economic agenda is working. But instead of taking the steps we need to strengthen the standing of working families, the Republican budgets for fiscal year (FY) 2016 would return our economy to the same top-down economics that has failed us before: cutting taxes for millionaires and billionaires, while slashing investments in the middle class that we need to grow the economy, like education, job training, and manufacturing. The Republican proposals stand in stark contrast to the President's FY 2016 Budget, which would bring middle class economics into the 21st Century. A state-by-state breakdown of this contrast, including how the Republican budgets affect Rhode Island, can be found in a report released today here: http://go.wh.gov/RoNU1j.

The President's Budget builds on the progress we've made and shows what we can do if we invest in America's future and commit to an economy that rewards hard work, generates rising incomes, and allows everyone to share in the prosperity of a growing America. It lays out a strategy to strengthen our middle class and help America's hard-working families get ahead in a time of relentless economic and technological change. And it makes the critical investments needed to accelerate and sustain economic growth in the long run, including in research, education, training, and infrastructure.

Republicans have chosen different priorities. Yet again, they are seeking to balance the budget on the backs of the middle class, while cutting taxes for the wealthy and well-connected. They still won't say where many of their spending cuts come from. But they are clear that their budgets would continue the harmful cuts known as sequestration in 2016, threatening economic growth, cutting programs middle-class families count on, and attempting to fund national security through irresponsible budget gimmicks. Their budgets slash domestic investments that support the middle-class even more significantly after 2016, along with programs that serve the most vulnerable Americans. House Republicans would end Medicare as we know it, transforming it from a guarantee seniors can count on into a voucher program. After five years of the Affordable Care Act, more than 16 million people have gained coverage. Yet once again, the Republican budgets propose to repeal the Affordable Care Act's coverage expansions.

The choice could not be more clear or the consequences more stark. Thanks to President Obama and the resilience of the American people, the economy is growing

again. The Republican budgets would put that growth at risk and limit opportunity for the middle-class and those seeking to join it.

In Rhode Island, the Republican budgets would[i]:

Cut Taxes for Millionaires and Raise Taxes for Working Families and Students:
While claiming to prioritize fiscal responsibility, the Republican budgets would not ask the wealthy to contribute a single dollar to deficit reduction, and the proposals specified in the House budget would cut taxes for millionaires by an average of at least $50,000. Meanwhile, the Republican budgets do nothing to prevent tax increases averaging $1,100 for 12 million families and students paying for college and $900 for 16 million working families with children. In 2015, 42,000 Rhode Island families will receive a total of $37 million in tax cuts from improvements to pro-work tax credits that would expire after 2017 under the Republican budgets.

Eliminate Affordable Health Care: The Affordable Care Act is working. After five years of the Affordable Care Act, more than 16 million people have gained coverage. Yet once again, the Republican budgets propose to repeal the Affordable Care Act's coverage expansions, taking away health insurance from millions of people. In particular, the Republican budgets would eliminate coverage for 31,000 Rhode Island residents who have newly signed up for coverage or re-enrolled through the Marketplaces. Some of these individuals would become uninsured while others would end up with worse or less affordable coverage.

Raise Health Care Costs for Seniors: 16,300 Rhode Island seniors and people with disabilities benefited by an average of $820 from the closure of the Medicare Part D prescription drug donut hole in 2014 alone. Under the Republican plan to repeal the Affordable Care Act, at least that many would likely have to pay more for needed medications in future years. The House budget would also end Medicare as we know it, replacing guaranteed access to the traditional Medicare program with a voucher program, risking a death spiral in traditional Medicare.

Slash Investments in the Middle Class: Under the Republican budgets, both non-defense and base defense discretionary funding in 2016 would be at the lowest real levels in a decade. Compared to the President's Budget, if the Republican budgets were to take effect, these are just some of the impacts on Rhode Island:

- **Head Start:** 120 fewer children in Rhode Island would have access to Head Start services, representing a permanently missed opportunity to help these children enter elementary school ready to succeed.
- **Teachers and Schools:** Rhode Island would receive $4.2 million less funding for disadvantaged students, an amount that is enough to fund about 10 schools, 60 teacher and aide jobs, and 4,000 students.

- **Education for Children with Disabilities:** Rhode Island would receive $1.2 million less funding to provide educational opportunities for students with disabilities, representing an approximately 2.8 percent cut and shifting the burden for meeting these children's needs to Rhode Island and its local communities.
- **Job Training and Employment Services:** 8,300 fewer Rhode Island residents would receive job training and employment services, including help finding jobs and skills training.
- **Affordable Housing**: Rhode Island would receive approximately $8.0 million less in Federal funding, resulting in 610 fewer families receiving Housing Choice Vouchers, which enable very low-income families to afford decent, safe, and sanitary housing in the private market.

Balances Only with Gimmicks and Deep Cuts to Programs that Serve the Most Vulnerable and Help Expand Opportunity. On top of their cuts to middle-class investments and the ACA, the Republican budgets would cut:

- **Pell Grants:** Republican reductions to Pell would reduce financial aid for the 31,000 Rhode Island students who rely on Pell grants to afford college.
- **Medicaid:** The House Republican proposal to block grant Medicaid would cut Federal funding to Rhode Island by approximately $4.6 billion over ten years, impacting children, seniors, and people with disabilities who rely on Medicaid.
- **Supplemental Nutrition Assistance Program (SNAP):** House Republican proposals to block grant and slash SNAP would cut nutrition aid in Rhode Island by an estimated $400 million over a five year period (2021-2025), jeopardizing nutrition assistance for the 179,000 Rhode Island residents who receive SNAP to help them put food on the table.

Fails to Address Our Crumbling Infrastructure: Republican budgets lack a real plan to address the looming expiration and insolvency of the Highway Trust Fund. Through the Highway Trust Fund, in FY 2014 the Federal Government obligated $222.1 million to Rhode Island through the Federal Aid Highways program for highway planning and construction and over $72.6 million through Transit Formula Grants that support our Nation's mass transit systems.

###

i. Numbers are rounded. For a description of how impacts were calculated, see http://go.wh.gov/RoNU1j

THE WHITE HOUSE

Office of the Press Secretary

FOR IMMEDIATE RELEASE

March 24, 2015

FACT SHEET: Republican Budget Resolutions: Same Failed Top-Down Economics for South Carolina

With more than 12 million private-sector jobs created over the last 60 months, it is clear that the President's middle class economic agenda is working. But instead of taking the steps we need to strengthen the standing of working families, the Republican budgets for fiscal year (FY) 2016 would return our economy to the same top-down economics that has failed us before: cutting taxes for millionaires and billionaires, while slashing investments in the middle class that we need to grow the economy, like education, job training, and manufacturing. The Republican proposals stand in stark contrast to the President's FY 2016 Budget, which would bring middle class economics into the 21st Century. A state-by-state breakdown of this contrast, including how the Republican budgets affect South Carolina, can be found in a report released today here: http://go.wh.gov/RoNU1j.

The President's Budget builds on the progress we've made and shows what we can do if we invest in America's future and commit to an economy that rewards hard work, generates rising incomes, and allows everyone to share in the prosperity of a growing America. It lays out a strategy to strengthen our middle class and help America's hard-working families get ahead in a time of relentless economic and technological change. And it makes the critical investments needed to accelerate and sustain economic growth in the long run, including in research, education, training, and infrastructure.

Republicans have chosen different priorities. Yet again, they are seeking to balance the budget on the backs of the middle class, while cutting taxes for the wealthy and well-connected. They still won't say where many of their spending cuts come from. But they are clear that their budgets would continue the harmful cuts known as sequestration in 2016, threatening economic growth, cutting programs middle-class families count on, and attempting to fund national security through irresponsible budget gimmicks. Their budgets slash domestic investments that support the middle-class even more significantly after 2016, along with programs that serve the most vulnerable Americans. House Republicans would end Medicare as we know it, transforming it from a guarantee seniors can count on into a voucher program. After five years of the Affordable Care Act, more than 16 million people have gained coverage. Yet once again, the Republican budgets propose to repeal the Affordable Care Act's coverage expansions.

The choice could not be more clear or the consequences more stark. Thanks to President Obama and the resilience of the American people, the economy is growing

again. The Republican budgets would put that growth at risk and limit opportunity for the middle-class and those seeking to join it.

In South Carolina, the Republican budgets would[i]:

Cut Taxes for Millionaires and Raise Taxes for Working Families and Students: While claiming to prioritize fiscal responsibility, the Republican budgets would not ask the wealthy to contribute a single dollar to deficit reduction, and the proposals specified in the House budget would cut taxes for millionaires by an average of at least $50,000. Meanwhile, the Republican budgets do nothing to prevent tax increases averaging $1,100 for 12 million families and students paying for college and $900 for 16 million working families with children. In 2015, 279,000 South Carolina families will receive a total of $253 million in tax cuts from improvements to pro-work tax credits that would expire after 2017 under the Republican budgets.

Eliminate Affordable Health Care: The Affordable Care Act is working. After five years of the Affordable Care Act, more than 16 million people have gained coverage. Yet once again, the Republican budgets propose to repeal the Affordable Care Act's coverage expansions, taking away health insurance from millions of people. In particular, the Republican budgets would eliminate coverage for 210,000 South Carolina residents who have newly signed up for coverage or re-enrolled through the Marketplaces. Some of these individuals would become uninsured while others would end up with worse or less affordable coverage.

Raise Health Care Costs for Seniors: 98,900 South Carolina seniors and people with disabilities benefited by an average of $970 from the closure of the Medicare Part D prescription drug donut hole in 2014 alone. Under the Republican plan to repeal the Affordable Care Act, at least that many would likely have to pay more for needed medications in future years. The House budget would also end Medicare as we know it, replacing guaranteed access to the traditional Medicare program with a voucher program, risking a death spiral in traditional Medicare.

Slash Investments in the Middle Class: Under the Republican budgets, both non-defense and base defense discretionary funding in 2016 would be at the lowest real levels in a decade. Compared to the President's Budget, if the Republican budgets were to take effect, these are just some of the impacts on South Carolina:

- **Head Start:** 460 fewer children in South Carolina would have access to Head Start services, representing a permanently missed opportunity to help these children enter elementary school ready to succeed.
- **Teachers and Schools:** South Carolina would receive $19.9 million less funding for disadvantaged students, an amount that is enough to fund about 40 schools, 270 teacher and aide jobs, and 24,000 students.

- **Education for Children with Disabilities:** South Carolina would receive $5.0 million less funding to provide educational opportunities for students with disabilities, representing an approximately 2.8 percent cut and shifting the burden for meeting these children's needs to South Carolina and its local communities.
- **Job Training and Employment Services:** 30,600 fewer South Carolina residents would receive job training and employment services, including help finding jobs and skills training.
- **Affordable Housing**: South Carolina would receive approximately $13.7 million less in Federal funding, resulting in 1,510 fewer families receiving Housing Choice Vouchers, which enable very low-income families to afford decent, safe, and sanitary housing in the private market.
- **National Parks:** Construction and renovation projects would be prevented or delayed at Fort Sumter National Monument.

Balances Only with Gimmicks and Deep Cuts to Programs that Serve the Most Vulnerable and Help Expand Opportunity. On top of their cuts to middle-class investments and the ACA, the Republican budgets would cut:

- **Pell Grants:** Republican reductions to Pell would reduce financial aid for the 115,000 South Carolina students who rely on Pell grants to afford college.
- **Medicaid:** The House Republican proposal to block grant Medicaid would cut Federal funding to South Carolina by approximately $12.3 billion over ten years, impacting children, seniors, and people with disabilities who rely on Medicaid.
- **Supplemental Nutrition Assistance Program (SNAP):** House Republican proposals to block grant and slash SNAP would cut nutrition aid in South Carolina by an estimated $2 billion over a five year period (2021-2025), jeopardizing nutrition assistance for the 835,000 South Carolina residents who receive SNAP to help them put food on the table.

Fails to Address Our Crumbling Infrastructure: Republican budgets lack a real plan to address the looming expiration and insolvency of the Highway Trust Fund. Through the Highway Trust Fund, in FY 2014 the Federal Government obligated $671.3 million to South Carolina through the Federal Aid Highways program for highway planning and construction and over $38.6 million through Transit Formula Grants that support our Nation's mass transit systems.

###

i. Numbers are rounded. For a description of how impacts were calculated, see http://go.wh.gov/RoNUIj

FOR IMMEDIATE RELEASE
March 24, 2015

FACT SHEET: Republican Budget Resolutions: Same Failed Top-Down Economics for South Dakota

With more than 12 million private-sector jobs created over the last 60 months, it is clear that the President's middle class economic agenda is working. But instead of taking the steps we need to strengthen the standing of working families, the Republican budgets for fiscal year (FY) 2016 would return our economy to the same top-down economics that has failed us before: cutting taxes for millionaires and billionaires, while slashing investments in the middle class that we need to grow the economy, like education, job training, and manufacturing. The Republican proposals stand in stark contrast to the President's FY 2016 Budget, which would bring middle class economics into the 21st Century. A state-by-state breakdown of this contrast, including how the Republican budgets affect South Dakota, can be found in a report released today here: http://go.wh.gov/RoNU1j.

The President's Budget builds on the progress we've made and shows what we can do if we invest in America's future and commit to an economy that rewards hard work, generates rising incomes, and allows everyone to share in the prosperity of a growing America. It lays out a strategy to strengthen our middle class and help America's hard-working families get ahead in a time of relentless economic and technological change. And it makes the critical investments needed to accelerate and sustain economic growth in the long run, including in research, education, training, and infrastructure.

Republicans have chosen different priorities. Yet again, they are seeking to balance the budget on the backs of the middle class, while cutting taxes for the wealthy and well-connected. They still won't say where many of their spending cuts come from. But they are clear that their budgets would continue the harmful cuts known as sequestration in 2016, threatening economic growth, cutting programs middle-class families count on, and attempting to fund national security through irresponsible budget gimmicks. Their budgets slash domestic investments that support the middle-class even more significantly after 2016, along with programs that serve the most vulnerable Americans. House Republicans would end Medicare as we know it, transforming it from a guarantee seniors can count on into a voucher program. After five years of the Affordable Care Act, more than 16 million people have gained coverage. Yet once again, the Republican budgets propose to repeal the Affordable Care Act's coverage expansions.

The choice could not be more clear or the consequences more stark. Thanks to President Obama and the resilience of the American people, the economy is growing

again. The Republican budgets would put that growth at risk and limit opportunity for the middle-class and those seeking to join it.

In South Dakota, the Republican budgets would[i]:

Cut Taxes for Millionaires and Raise Taxes for Working Families and Students: While claiming to prioritize fiscal responsibility, the Republican budgets would not ask the wealthy to contribute a single dollar to deficit reduction, and the proposals specified in the House budget would cut taxes for millionaires by an average of at least $50,000. Meanwhile, the Republican budgets do nothing to prevent tax increases averaging $1,100 for 12 million families and students paying for college and $900 for 16 million working families with children. In 2015, 36,000 South Dakota families will receive a total of $31 million in tax cuts from improvements to pro-work tax credits that would expire after 2017 under the Republican budgets.

Eliminate Affordable Health Care: The Affordable Care Act is working. After five years of the Affordable Care Act, more than 16 million people have gained coverage. Yet once again, the Republican budgets propose to repeal the Affordable Care Act's coverage expansions, taking away health insurance from millions of people. In particular, the Republican budgets would eliminate coverage for 21,000 South Dakota residents who have newly signed up for coverage or re-enrolled through the Marketplaces. Some of these individuals would become uninsured while others would end up with worse or less affordable coverage.

Raise Health Care Costs for Seniors: 13,100 South Dakota seniors and people with disabilities benefited by an average of $800 from the closure of the Medicare Part D prescription drug donut hole in 2014 alone. Under the Republican plan to repeal the Affordable Care Act, at least that many would likely have to pay more for needed medications in future years. The House budget would also end Medicare as we know it, replacing guaranteed access to the traditional Medicare program with a voucher program, risking a death spiral in traditional Medicare.

Slash Investments in the Middle Class: Under the Republican budgets, both non-defense and base defense discretionary funding in 2016 would be at the lowest real levels in a decade. Compared to the President's Budget, if the Republican budgets were to take effect, these are just some of the impacts on South Dakota:

- **Head Start:** 100 fewer children in South Dakota would have access to Head Start services, representing a permanently missed opportunity to help these children enter elementary school ready to succeed.
- **Teachers and Schools:** South Dakota would receive $4.1 million less funding for disadvantaged students, an amount that is enough to fund about 30 schools, 60 teacher and aide jobs, and 4,000 students.

- **Education for Children with Disabilities:** South Dakota would receive $1.6 million less funding to provide educational opportunities for students with disabilities, representing an approximately 4.5 percent cut and shifting the burden for meeting these children's needs to South Dakota and its local communities.
- **Job Training and Employment Services:** 15,700 fewer South Dakota residents would receive job training and employment services, including help finding jobs and skills training.
- **Affordable Housing**: South Dakota would receive approximately $2.7 million less in Federal funding, resulting in 330 fewer families receiving Housing Choice Vouchers, which enable very low-income families to afford decent, safe, and sanitary housing in the private market.
- **National Parks:** Construction and renovation projects would be prevented or delayed at three national parks in South Dakota: Badlands National Park, Mount Rushmore National Memorial, and Wine Cave National Park.

Balances Only with Gimmicks and Deep Cuts to Programs that Serve the Most Vulnerable and Help Expand Opportunity. On top of their cuts to middle-class investments and the ACA, the Republican budgets would cut:

- **Pell Grants:** Republican reductions to Pell would reduce financial aid for the 25,000 South Dakota students who rely on Pell grants to afford college.
- **Medicaid:** The House Republican proposal to block grant Medicaid would cut Federal funding to South Dakota by approximately $1.5 billion over ten years, impacting children, seniors, and people with disabilities who rely on Medicaid.
- **Supplemental Nutrition Assistance Program (SNAP):** House Republican proposals to block grant and slash SNAP would cut nutrition aid in South Dakota by an estimated $200 million over a five year period (2021-2025), jeopardizing nutrition assistance for the 101,000 South Dakota residents who receive SNAP to help them put food on the table.

Fails to Address Our Crumbling Infrastructure: Republican budgets lack a real plan to address the looming expiration and insolvency of the Highway Trust Fund. Through the Highway Trust Fund, in FY 2014 the Federal Government obligated $315.5 million to South Dakota through the Federal Aid Highways program for highway planning and construction and over $20.4 million through Transit Formula Grants that support our Nation's mass transit systems.

i. Numbers are rounded. For a description of how impacts were calculated, see http://go.wh.gov/RoNU1j

THE WHITE HOUSE
Office of the Press Secretary

FOR IMMEDIATE RELEASE
March 24, 2015

FACT SHEET: Republican Budget Resolutions: Same Failed Top-Down Economics for Tennessee

With more than 12 million private-sector jobs created over the last 60 months, it is clear that the President's middle class economic agenda is working. But instead of taking the steps we need to strengthen the standing of working families, the Republican budgets for fiscal year (FY) 2016 would return our economy to the same top-down economics that has failed us before: cutting taxes for millionaires and billionaires, while slashing investments in the middle class that we need to grow the economy, like education, job training, and manufacturing. The Republican proposals stand in stark contrast to the President's FY 2016 Budget, which would bring middle class economics into the 21st Century. A state-by-state breakdown of this contrast, including how the Republican budgets affect Tennessee, can be found in a report released today here: http://go.wh.gov/RoNU1j.

The President's Budget builds on the progress we've made and shows what we can do if we invest in America's future and commit to an economy that rewards hard work, generates rising incomes, and allows everyone to share in the prosperity of a growing America. It lays out a strategy to strengthen our middle class and help America's hard-working families get ahead in a time of relentless economic and technological change. And it makes the critical investments needed to accelerate and sustain economic growth in the long run, including in research, education, training, and infrastructure.

Republicans have chosen different priorities. Yet again, they are seeking to balance the budget on the backs of the middle class, while cutting taxes for the wealthy and well-connected. They still won't say where many of their spending cuts come from. But they are clear that their budgets would continue the harmful cuts known as sequestration in 2016, threatening economic growth, cutting programs middle-class families count on, and attempting to fund national security through irresponsible budget gimmicks. Their budgets slash domestic investments that support the middle-class even more significantly after 2016, along with programs that serve the most vulnerable Americans. House Republicans would end Medicare as we know it, transforming it from a guarantee seniors can count on into a voucher program. After five years of the Affordable Care Act, more than 16 million people have gained coverage. Yet once again, the Republican budgets propose to repeal the Affordable Care Act's coverage expansions.

The choice could not be more clear or the consequences more stark. Thanks to President Obama and the resilience of the American people, the economy is growing

again. The Republican budgets would put that growth at risk and limit opportunity for the middle-class and those seeking to join it.

In Tennessee, the Republican budgets would[i]:

Cut Taxes for Millionaires and Raise Taxes for Working Families and Students: While claiming to prioritize fiscal responsibility, the Republican budgets would not ask the wealthy to contribute a single dollar to deficit reduction, and the proposals specified in the House budget would cut taxes for millionaires by an average of at least $50,000. Meanwhile, the Republican budgets do nothing to prevent tax increases averaging $1,100 for 12 million families and students paying for college and $900 for 16 million working families with children. In 2015, 383,000 Tennessee families will receive a total of $341 million in tax cuts from improvements to pro-work tax credits that would expire after 2017 under the Republican budgets.

Eliminate Affordable Health Care: The Affordable Care Act is working. After five years of the Affordable Care Act, more than 16 million people have gained coverage. Yet once again, the Republican budgets propose to repeal the Affordable Care Act's coverage expansions, taking away health insurance from millions of people. In particular, the Republican budgets would eliminate coverage for 231,000 Tennessee residents who have newly signed up for coverage or re-enrolled through the Marketplaces. Some of these individuals would become uninsured while others would end up with worse or less affordable coverage.

Raise Health Care Costs for Seniors: 112,100 Tennessee seniors and people with disabilities benefited by an average of $840 from the closure of the Medicare Part D prescription drug donut hole in 2014 alone. Under the Republican plan to repeal the Affordable Care Act, at least that many would likely have to pay more for needed medications in future years. The House budget would also end Medicare as we know it, replacing guaranteed access to the traditional Medicare program with a voucher program, risking a death spiral in traditional Medicare.

Slash Investments in the Middle Class: Under the Republican budgets, both non-defense and base defense discretionary funding in 2016 would be at the lowest real levels in a decade. Compared to the President's Budget, if the Republican budgets were to take effect, these are just some of the impacts on Tennessee:

- **Head Start:** 630 fewer children in Tennessee would have access to Head Start services, representing a permanently missed opportunity to help these children enter elementary school ready to succeed.
- **Teachers and Schools:** Tennessee would receive $25.0 million less funding for disadvantaged students, an amount that is enough to fund about 90 schools, 340 teacher and aide jobs, and 45,000 students.

- **Education for Children with Disabilities:** Tennessee would receive $6.8 million less funding to provide educational opportunities for students with disabilities, representing an approximately 2.8 percent cut and shifting the burden for meeting these children's needs to Tennessee and its local communities.
- **Job Training and Employment Services:** 42,800 fewer Tennessee residents would receive job training and employment services, including help finding jobs and skills training.
- **Affordable Housing**: Tennessee would receive approximately $20.3 million less in Federal funding, resulting in 2,190 fewer families receiving Housing Choice Vouchers, which enable very low-income families to afford decent, safe, and sanitary housing in the private market.
- **National Parks:** Construction and renovation projects would be prevented or delayed at four national parks in Tennessee: Andrew Johnson National Historic Site, Great Smoky Mountains National Park, Appalachian National Scenic Trail, and Obed Wild and Scenic River.

Balances Only with Gimmicks and Deep Cuts to Programs that Serve the Most Vulnerable and Help Expand Opportunity. On top of their cuts to middle-class investments and the ACA, the Republican budgets would cut:

- **Pell Grants:** Republican reductions to Pell would reduce financial aid for the 164,000 Tennessee students who rely on Pell grants to afford college.
- **Medicaid:** The House Republican proposal to block grant Medicaid would cut Federal funding to Tennessee by approximately $19.6 billion over ten years, impacting children, seniors, and people with disabilities who rely on Medicaid.
- **Supplemental Nutrition Assistance Program (SNAP):** House Republican proposals to block grant and slash SNAP would cut nutrition aid in Tennessee by an estimated $3.1 billion over a five year period (2021-2025), jeopardizing nutrition assistance for the 1,313,000 Tennessee residents who receive SNAP to help them put food on the table.

Fails to Address Our Crumbling Infrastructure: Republican budgets lack a real plan to address the looming expiration and insolvency of the Highway Trust Fund. Through the Highway Trust Fund, in FY 2014 the Federal Government obligated $799.0 million to Tennessee through the Federal Aid Highways program for highway planning and construction and over $115.8 million through Transit Formula Grants that support our Nation's mass transit systems.

i. Numbers are rounded. For a description of how impacts were calculated, see http://go.wh.gov/RoNU1j

THE WHITE HOUSE
Office of the Press Secretary

FOR IMMEDIATE RELEASE
March 24, 2015

FACT SHEET: Republican Budget Resolutions: Same Failed Top-Down Economics for Texas

With more than 12 million private-sector jobs created over the last 60 months, it is clear that the President's middle class economic agenda is working. But instead of taking the steps we need to strengthen the standing of working families, the Republican budgets for fiscal year (FY) 2016 would return our economy to the same top-down economics that has failed us before: cutting taxes for millionaires and billionaires, while slashing investments in the middle class that we need to grow the economy, like education, job training, and manufacturing. The Republican proposals stand in stark contrast to the President's FY 2016 Budget, which would bring middle class economics into the 21st Century. A state-by-state breakdown of this contrast, including how the Republican budgets affect Texas, can be found in a report released today here: http://go.wh.gov/RoNU1j.

The President's Budget builds on the progress we've made and shows what we can do if we invest in America's future and commit to an economy that rewards hard work, generates rising incomes, and allows everyone to share in the prosperity of a growing America. It lays out a strategy to strengthen our middle class and help America's hard-working families get ahead in a time of relentless economic and technological change. And it makes the critical investments needed to accelerate and sustain economic growth in the long run, including in research, education, training, and infrastructure.

Republicans have chosen different priorities. Yet again, they are seeking to balance the budget on the backs of the middle class, while cutting taxes for the wealthy and well-connected. They still won't say where many of their spending cuts come from. But they are clear that their budgets would continue the harmful cuts known as sequestration in 2016, threatening economic growth, cutting programs middle-class families count on, and attempting to fund national security through irresponsible budget gimmicks. Their budgets slash domestic investments that support the middle-class even more significantly after 2016, along with programs that serve the most vulnerable Americans. House Republicans would end Medicare as we know it, transforming it from a guarantee seniors can count on into a voucher program. After five years of the Affordable Care Act, more than 16 million people have gained coverage. Yet once again, the Republican budgets propose to repeal the Affordable Care Act's coverage expansions.

The choice could not be more clear or the consequences more stark. Thanks to President Obama and the resilience of the American people, the economy is growing

again. The Republican budgets would put that growth at risk and limit opportunity for the middle-class and those seeking to join it.

In Texas, the Republican budgets would[i]:

Cut Taxes for Millionaires and Raise Taxes for Working Families and Students: While claiming to prioritize fiscal responsibility, the Republican budgets would not ask the wealthy to contribute a single dollar to deficit reduction, and the proposals specified in the House budget would cut taxes for millionaires by an average of at least $50,000. Meanwhile, the Republican budgets do nothing to prevent tax increases averaging $1,100 for 12 million families and students paying for college and $900 for 16 million working families with children. In 2015, nearly 1.6 million Texas families will receive a total of $1.5 billion in tax cuts from improvements to pro-work tax credits that would expire after 2017 under the Republican budgets.

Eliminate Affordable Health Care: The Affordable Care Act is working. After five years of the Affordable Care Act, more than 16 million people have gained coverage. Yet once again, the Republican budgets propose to repeal the Affordable Care Act's coverage expansions, taking away health insurance from millions of people. In particular, the Republican budgets would eliminate coverage for more than 1.2 million Texas residents who have newly signed up for coverage or re-enrolled through the Marketplaces. Some of these individuals would become uninsured while others would end up with worse or less affordable coverage.

Raise Health Care Costs for Seniors: 345,500 Texas seniors and people with disabilities benefited by an average of $950 from the closure of the Medicare Part D prescription drug donut hole in 2014 alone. Under the Republican plan to repeal the Affordable Care Act, at least that many would likely have to pay more for needed medications in future years. The House budget would also end Medicare as we know it, replacing guaranteed access to the traditional Medicare program with a voucher program, risking a death spiral in traditional Medicare.

Slash Investments in the Middle Class: Under the Republican budgets, both non-defense and base defense discretionary funding in 2016 would be at the lowest real levels in a decade. Compared to the President's Budget, if the Republican budgets were to take effect, these are just some of the impacts on Texas:

- **Head Start:** 2,630 fewer children in Texas would have access to Head Start services, representing a permanently missed opportunity to help these children enter elementary school ready to succeed.
- **Teachers and Schools:** Texas would receive $112.9 million less funding for disadvantaged students, an amount that is enough to fund about 470 schools, 1,550 teacher and aide jobs, and 278,000 students.

- **Education for Children with Disabilities:** Texas would receive $29.2 million less funding to provide educational opportunities for students with disabilities, representing an approximately 2.9 percent cut and shifting the burden for meeting these children's needs to Texas and its local communities.
- **Job Training and Employment Services:** 163,900 fewer Texas residents would receive job training and employment services, including help finding jobs and skills training.
- **Affordable Housing:** Texas would receive approximately $98.2 million less in Federal funding, resulting in 8,920 fewer families receiving Housing Choice Vouchers, which enable very low-income families to afford decent, safe, and sanitary housing in the private market.
- **National Parks:** Construction and renovation projects would be prevented or delayed at two national parks in Texas: Guadalupe Mountains National Park and Lyndon B. Johnson National Historical Park.

Balances Only with Gimmicks and Deep Cuts to Programs that Serve the Most Vulnerable and Help Expand Opportunity. On top of their cuts to middle-class investments and the ACA, the Republican budgets would cut:

- **Pell Grants:** Republican reductions to Pell would reduce financial aid for the 605,000 Texas students who rely on Pell grants to afford college.
- **Medicaid:** The House Republican proposal to block grant Medicaid would cut Federal funding to Texas by approximately $60.9 billion over ten years, impacting children, seniors, and people with disabilities who rely on Medicaid.
- **Supplemental Nutrition Assistance Program (SNAP):** House Republican proposals to block grant and slash SNAP would cut nutrition aid in Texas by an estimated $8.5 billion over a five year period (2021-2025), jeopardizing nutrition assistance for the 3,853,000 Texas residents who receive SNAP to help them put food on the table.

Fails to Address Our Crumbling Infrastructure: Republican budgets lack a real plan to address the looming expiration and insolvency of the Highway Trust Fund. Through the Highway Trust Fund, in FY 2014 the Federal Government obligated $3.6 billion to Texas through the Federal Aid Highways program for highway planning and construction and over $420.2 million through Transit Formula Grants that support our Nation's mass transit systems.

###

i. Numbers are rounded. For a description of how impacts were calculated, see http://go.wh.gov/RoNU1j

THE WHITE HOUSE
Office of the Press Secretary

FOR IMMEDIATE RELEASE
March 24, 2015

FACT SHEET: Republican Budget Resolutions: Same Failed Top-Down Economics for Utah

With more than 12 million private-sector jobs created over the last 60 months, it is clear that the President's middle class economic agenda is working. But instead of taking the steps we need to strengthen the standing of working families, the Republican budgets for fiscal year (FY) 2016 would return our economy to the same top-down economics that has failed us before: cutting taxes for millionaires and billionaires, while slashing investments in the middle class that we need to grow the economy, like education, job training, and manufacturing. The Republican proposals stand in stark contrast to the President's FY 2016 Budget, which would bring middle class economics into the 21st Century. A state-by-state breakdown of this contrast, including how the Republican budgets affect Utah, can be found in a report released today here: http://go.wh.gov/RoNU1j.

The President's Budget builds on the progress we've made and shows what we can do if we invest in America's future and commit to an economy that rewards hard work, generates rising incomes, and allows everyone to share in the prosperity of a growing America. It lays out a strategy to strengthen our middle class and help America's hard-working families get ahead in a time of relentless economic and technological change. And it makes the critical investments needed to accelerate and sustain economic growth in the long run, including in research, education, training, and infrastructure.

Republicans have chosen different priorities. Yet again, they are seeking to balance the budget on the backs of the middle class, while cutting taxes for the wealthy and well-connected. They still won't say where many of their spending cuts come from. But they are clear that their budgets would continue the harmful cuts known as sequestration in 2016, threatening economic growth, cutting programs middle-class families count on, and attempting to fund national security through irresponsible budget gimmicks. Their budgets slash domestic investments that support the middle-class even more significantly after 2016, along with programs that serve the most vulnerable Americans. House Republicans would end Medicare as we know it, transforming it from a guarantee seniors can count on into a voucher program. After five years of the Affordable Care Act, more than 16 million people have gained coverage. Yet once again, the Republican budgets propose to repeal the Affordable Care Act's coverage expansions.

The choice could not be more clear or the consequences more stark. Thanks to President Obama and the resilience of the American people, the economy is growing

again. The Republican budgets would put that growth at risk and limit opportunity for the middle-class and those seeking to join it.

In Utah, the Republican budgets would[i]:

Cut Taxes for Millionaires and Raise Taxes for Working Families and Students: While claiming to prioritize fiscal responsibility, the Republican budgets would not ask the wealthy to contribute a single dollar to deficit reduction, and the proposals specified in the House budget would cut taxes for millionaires by an average of at least $50,000. Meanwhile, the Republican budgets do nothing to prevent tax increases averaging $1,100 for 12 million families and students paying for college and $900 for 16 million working families with children. In 2015, 147,000 Utah families will receive a total of $140 million in tax cuts from improvements to pro-work tax credits that would expire after 2017 under the Republican budgets.

Eliminate Affordable Health Care: The Affordable Care Act is working. After five years of the Affordable Care Act, more than 16 million people have gained coverage. Yet once again, the Republican budgets propose to repeal the Affordable Care Act's coverage expansions, taking away health insurance from millions of people. In particular, the Republican budgets would eliminate coverage for 141,000 Utah residents who have newly signed up for coverage or re-enrolled through the Marketplaces. Some of these individuals would become uninsured while others would end up with worse or less affordable coverage.

Raise Health Care Costs for Seniors: 27,200 Utah seniors and people with disabilities benefited by an average of $840 from the closure of the Medicare Part D prescription drug donut hole in 2014 alone. Under the Republican plan to repeal the Affordable Care Act, at least that many would likely have to pay more for needed medications in future years. The House budget would also end Medicare as we know it, replacing guaranteed access to the traditional Medicare program with a voucher program, risking a death spiral in traditional Medicare.

Slash Investments in the Middle Class: Under the Republican budgets, both non-defense and base defense discretionary funding in 2016 would be at the lowest real levels in a decade. Compared to the President's Budget, if the Republican budgets were to take effect, these are just some of the impacts on Utah:

- **Head Start:** 220 fewer children in Utah would have access to Head Start services, representing a permanently missed opportunity to help these children enter elementary school ready to succeed.
- **Teachers and Schools:** Utah would receive $7.9 million less funding for disadvantaged students, an amount that is enough to fund about 20 schools, 110 teacher and aide jobs, and 12,000 students.

- **Education for Children with Disabilities:** Utah would receive $5.1 million less funding to provide educational opportunities for students with disabilities, representing an approximately 4.5 percent cut and shifting the burden for meeting these children's needs to Utah and its local communities.
- **Job Training and Employment Services:** 21,400 fewer Utah residents would receive job training and employment services, including help finding jobs and skills training.
- **Affordable Housing**: Utah would receive approximately $6.9 million less in Federal funding, resulting in 710 fewer families receiving Housing Choice Vouchers, which enable very low-income families to afford decent, safe, and sanitary housing in the private market.
- **National Parks:** Construction and renovation projects would be prevented or delayed at six national parks in Utah: Bryce Canyon National Park, Canyonlands National Park, Capitol Reef National Park, Cedar Breaks National Monument, Hovenweep National Memorial, and Timpanogos Cave National Monument.

Balances Only with Gimmicks and Deep Cuts to Programs that Serve the Most Vulnerable and Help Expand Opportunity. On top of their cuts to middle-class investments and the ACA, the Republican budgets would cut:

- **Pell Grants:** Republican reductions to Pell would reduce financial aid for the 115,000 Utah students who rely on Pell grants to afford college.
- **Medicaid:** The House Republican proposal to block grant Medicaid would cut Federal funding to Utah by approximately $4.9 billion over ten years, impacting children, seniors, and people with disabilities who rely on Medicaid.
- **Supplemental Nutrition Assistance Program (SNAP):** House Republican proposals to block grant and slash SNAP would cut nutrition aid in Utah by an estimated $500 million over a five year period (2021-2025), jeopardizing nutrition assistance for the 230,000 Utah residents who receive SNAP to help them put food on the table.

Fails to Address Our Crumbling Infrastructure: Republican budgets lack a real plan to address the looming expiration and insolvency of the Highway Trust Fund. Through the Highway Trust Fund, in FY 2014 the Federal Government obligated $346.0 million to Utah through the Federal Aid Highways program for highway planning and construction and over $57.4 million through Transit Formula Grants that support our Nation's mass transit systems.

###

i. Numbers are rounded. For a description of how impacts were calculated, see http://go.wh.gov/RoNU1j

FOR IMMEDIATE RELEASE
March 24, 2015

FACT SHEET: Republican Budget Resolutions: Same Failed Top-Down Economics for Vermont

With more than 12 million private-sector jobs created over the last 60 months, it is clear that the President's middle class economic agenda is working. But instead of taking the steps we need to strengthen the standing of working families, the Republican budgets for fiscal year (FY) 2016 would return our economy to the same top-down economics that has failed us before: cutting taxes for millionaires and billionaires, while slashing investments in the middle class that we need to grow the economy, like education, job training, and manufacturing. The Republican proposals stand in stark contrast to the President's FY 2016 Budget, which would bring middle class economics into the 21st Century. A state-by-state breakdown of this contrast, including how the Republican budgets affect Vermont, can be found in a report released today here: http://go.wh.gov/RoNU1j.

The President's Budget builds on the progress we've made and shows what we can do if we invest in America's future and commit to an economy that rewards hard work, generates rising incomes, and allows everyone to share in the prosperity of a growing America. It lays out a strategy to strengthen our middle class and help America's hard-working families get ahead in a time of relentless economic and technological change. And it makes the critical investments needed to accelerate and sustain economic growth in the long run, including in research, education, training, and infrastructure.

Republicans have chosen different priorities. Yet again, they are seeking to balance the budget on the backs of the middle class, while cutting taxes for the wealthy and well-connected. They still won't say where many of their spending cuts come from. But they are clear that their budgets would continue the harmful cuts known as sequestration in 2016, threatening economic growth, cutting programs middle-class families count on, and attempting to fund national security through irresponsible budget gimmicks. Their budgets slash domestic investments that support the middle-class even more significantly after 2016, along with programs that serve the most vulnerable Americans. House Republicans would end Medicare as we know it, transforming it from a guarantee seniors can count on into a voucher program. After five years of the Affordable Care Act, more than 16 million people have gained coverage. Yet once again, the Republican budgets propose to repeal the Affordable Care Act's coverage expansions.

The choice could not be more clear or the consequences more stark. Thanks to President Obama and the resilience of the American people, the economy is growing

again. The Republican budgets would put that growth at risk and limit opportunity for the middle-class and those seeking to join it.

In Vermont, the Republican budgets would[i]:

Cut Taxes for Millionaires and Raise Taxes for Working Families and Students: While claiming to prioritize fiscal responsibility, the Republican budgets would not ask the wealthy to contribute a single dollar to deficit reduction, and the proposals specified in the House budget would cut taxes for millionaires by an average of at least $50,000. Meanwhile, the Republican budgets do nothing to prevent tax increases averaging $1,100 for 12 million families and students paying for college and $900 for 16 million working families with children. In 2015, 23,000 Vermont families will receive a total of $19 million in tax cuts from improvements to pro-work tax credits that would expire after 2017 under the Republican budgets.

Eliminate Affordable Health Care: The Affordable Care Act is working. After five years of the Affordable Care Act, more than 16 million people have gained coverage. Yet once again, the Republican budgets propose to repeal the Affordable Care Act's coverage expansions, taking away health insurance from millions of people. In particular, the Republican budgets would eliminate coverage for 32,000 Vermont residents who have newly signed up for coverage or re-enrolled through the Marketplaces. Some of these individuals would become uninsured while others would end up with worse or less affordable coverage.

Raise Health Care Costs for Seniors: 9,700 Vermont seniors and people with disabilities benefited by an average of $950 from the closure of the Medicare Part D prescription drug donut hole in 2014 alone. Under the Republican plan to repeal the Affordable Care Act, at least that many would likely have to pay more for needed medications in future years. The House budget would also end Medicare as we know it, replacing guaranteed access to the traditional Medicare program with a voucher program, risking a death spiral in traditional Medicare.

Slash Investments in the Middle Class: Under the Republican budgets, both non-defense and base defense discretionary funding in 2016 would be at the lowest real levels in a decade. Compared to the President's Budget, if the Republican budgets were to take effect, these are just some of the impacts on Vermont:

- **Head Start:** 70 fewer children in Vermont would have access to Head Start services, representing a permanently missed opportunity to help these children enter elementary school ready to succeed.
- **Teachers and Schools:** Vermont would receive $3.1 million less funding for disadvantaged students, an amount that is enough to fund about 20 schools, 40 teacher and aide jobs, and 4,000 students.

- **Education for Children with Disabilities:** Vermont would receive $1.3 million less funding to provide educational opportunities for students with disabilities, representing an approximately 4.5 percent cut and shifting the burden for meeting these children's needs to Vermont and its local communities.
- **Job Training and Employment Services:** 7,400 fewer Vermont residents would receive job training and employment services, including help finding jobs and skills training.
- **Affordable Housing**: Vermont would receive approximately $4.7 million less in Federal funding, resulting in 460 fewer families receiving Housing Choice Vouchers, which enable very low-income families to afford decent, safe, and sanitary housing in the private market.
- **National Parks:** Construction and renovation projects would be prevented or delayed at Marsh-Billings-Rockefeller National Historical Park.

Balances Only with Gimmicks and Deep Cuts to Programs that Serve the Most Vulnerable and Help Expand Opportunity. On top of their cuts to middle-class investments and the ACA, the Republican budgets would cut:

- **Pell Grants:** Republican reductions to Pell would reduce financial aid for the 12,000 Vermont students who rely on Pell grants to afford college.
- **Medicaid:** The House Republican proposal to block grant Medicaid would cut Federal funding to Vermont by approximately $2.9 billion over ten years, impacting children, seniors, and people with disabilities who rely on Medicaid.
- **Supplemental Nutrition Assistance Program (SNAP):** House Republican proposals to block grant and slash SNAP would cut nutrition aid in Vermont by an estimated $200 million over a five year period (2021-2025), jeopardizing nutrition assistance for the 93,000 Vermont residents who receive SNAP to help them put food on the table.

Fails to Address Our Crumbling Infrastructure: Republican budgets lack a real plan to address the looming expiration and insolvency of the Highway Trust Fund. Through the Highway Trust Fund, in FY 2014 the Federal Government obligated $210.3 million to Vermont through the Federal Aid Highways program for highway planning and construction and over $50.2 million through Transit Formula Grants that support our Nation's mass transit systems.

###

i. Numbers are rounded. For a description of how impacts were calculated, see http://go.wh.gov/RoNU1j

FOR IMMEDIATE RELEASE
March 24, 2015

FACT SHEET: Republican Budget Resolutions: Same Failed Top-Down Economics for Virginia

With more than 12 million private-sector jobs created over the last 60 months, it is clear that the President's middle class economic agenda is working. But instead of taking the steps we need to strengthen the standing of working families, the Republican budgets for fiscal year (FY) 2016 would return our economy to the same top-down economics that has failed us before: cutting taxes for millionaires and billionaires, while slashing investments in the middle class that we need to grow the economy, like education, job training, and manufacturing. The Republican proposals stand in stark contrast to the President's FY 2016 Budget, which would bring middle class economics into the 21st Century. A state-by-state breakdown of this contrast, including how the Republican budgets affect Virginia, can be found in a report released today here: http://go.wh.gov/RoNU1j.

The President's Budget builds on the progress we've made and shows what we can do if we invest in America's future and commit to an economy that rewards hard work, generates rising incomes, and allows everyone to share in the prosperity of a growing America. It lays out a strategy to strengthen our middle class and help America's hard-working families get ahead in a time of relentless economic and technological change. And it makes the critical investments needed to accelerate and sustain economic growth in the long run, including in research, education, training, and infrastructure.

Republicans have chosen different priorities. Yet again, they are seeking to balance the budget on the backs of the middle class, while cutting taxes for the wealthy and well-connected. They still won't say where many of their spending cuts come from. But they are clear that their budgets would continue the harmful cuts known as sequestration in 2016, threatening economic growth, cutting programs middle-class families count on, and attempting to fund national security through irresponsible budget gimmicks. Their budgets slash domestic investments that support the middle-class even more significantly after 2016, along with programs that serve the most vulnerable Americans. House Republicans would end Medicare as we know it, transforming it from a guarantee seniors can count on into a voucher program. After five years of the Affordable Care Act, more than 16 million people have gained coverage. Yet once again, the Republican budgets propose to repeal the Affordable Care Act's coverage expansions.

The choice could not be more clear or the consequences more stark. Thanks to President Obama and the resilience of the American people, the economy is growing

again. The Republican budgets would put that growth at risk and limit opportunity for the middle-class and those seeking to join it.

In Virginia, the Republican budgets would[i]:

Cut Taxes for Millionaires and Raise Taxes for Working Families and Students: While claiming to prioritize fiscal responsibility, the Republican budgets would not ask the wealthy to contribute a single dollar to deficit reduction, and the proposals specified in the House budget would cut taxes for millionaires by an average of at least $50,000. Meanwhile, the Republican budgets do nothing to prevent tax increases averaging $1,100 for 12 million families and students paying for college and $900 for 16 million working families with children. In 2015, 329,000 Virginia families will receive a total of $288 million in tax cuts from improvements to pro-work tax credits that would expire after 2017 under the Republican budgets.

Eliminate Affordable Health Care: The Affordable Care Act is working. After five years of the Affordable Care Act, more than 16 million people have gained coverage. Yet once again, the Republican budgets propose to repeal the Affordable Care Act's coverage expansions, taking away health insurance from millions of people. In particular, the Republican budgets would eliminate coverage for 385,000 Virginia residents who have newly signed up for coverage or re-enrolled through the Marketplaces. Some of these individuals would become uninsured while others would end up with worse or less affordable coverage.

Raise Health Care Costs for Seniors: 112,000 Virginia seniors and people with disabilities benefited by an average of $910 from the closure of the Medicare Part D prescription drug donut hole in 2014 alone. Under the Republican plan to repeal the Affordable Care Act, at least that many would likely have to pay more for needed medications in future years. The House budget would also end Medicare as we know it, replacing guaranteed access to the traditional Medicare program with a voucher program, risking a death spiral in traditional Medicare.

Slash Investments in the Middle Class: Under the Republican budgets, both non-defense and base defense discretionary funding in 2016 would be at the lowest real levels in a decade. Compared to the President's Budget, if the Republican budgets were to take effect, these are just some of the impacts on Virginia:

- **Head Start:** 540 fewer children in Virginia would have access to Head Start services, representing a permanently missed opportunity to help these children enter elementary school ready to succeed.
- **Teachers and Schools:** Virginia would receive $20.0 million less funding for disadvantaged students, an amount that is enough to fund about 60 schools, 280 teacher and aide jobs, and 21,000 students.

- **Education for Children with Disabilities:** Virginia would receive $8.1 million less funding to provide educational opportunities for students with disabilities, representing an approximately 2.8 percent cut and shifting the burden for meeting these children's needs to Virginia and its local communities.
- **Job Training and Employment Services:** 53,900 fewer Virginia residents would receive job training and employment services, including help finding jobs and skills training.
- **Affordable Housing**: Virginia would receive approximately $37.5 million less in Federal funding, resulting in 2,730 fewer families receiving Housing Choice Vouchers, which enable very low-income families to afford decent, safe, and sanitary housing in the private market.
- **National Parks:** Construction and renovation projects would be prevented or delayed at eight national parks in Virginia: Cedar Creek and Belle Grove National Historic Park, Colonial National Historic Park, Cumberland Gap National Historical Park, Fredericksburg and Spotsylvania National Military Park, Maggie L. Walker National Historic Site, Richmond National Battlefield Park, Shenandoah National Park, and Appalachian National Scenic Trail.

Balances Only with Gimmicks and Deep Cuts to Programs that Serve the Most Vulnerable and Help Expand Opportunity. On top of their cuts to middle-class investments and the ACA, the Republican budgets would cut:

- **Pell Grants:** Republican reductions to Pell would reduce financial aid for the 188,000 Virginia students who rely on Pell grants to afford college.
- **Medicaid:** The House Republican proposal to block grant Medicaid would cut Federal funding to Virginia by approximately $12.8 billion over ten years, impacting children, seniors, and people with disabilities who rely on Medicaid.
- **Supplemental Nutrition Assistance Program (SNAP):** House Republican proposals to block grant and slash SNAP would cut nutrition aid in Virginia by an estimated $2.1 billion over a five year period (2021-2025), jeopardizing nutrition assistance for the 919,000 Virginia residents who receive SNAP to help them put food on the table.

Fails to Address Our Crumbling Infrastructure: Republican budgets lack a real plan to address the looming expiration and insolvency of the Highway Trust Fund. Through the Highway Trust Fund, in FY 2014 the Federal Government obligated $974.5 million to Virginia through the Federal Aid Highways program for highway planning and construction and over $168.1 million through Transit Formula Grants that support our Nation's mass transit systems.

i. Numbers are rounded. For a description of how impacts were calculated, see http://go.wh.gov/RoNU1j

THE WHITE HOUSE
Office of the Press Secretary

FOR IMMEDIATE RELEASE
March 24, 2015

FACT SHEET: Republican Budget Resolutions: Same Failed Top-Down Economics for Washington

With more than 12 million private-sector jobs created over the last 60 months, it is clear that the President's middle class economic agenda is working. But instead of taking the steps we need to strengthen the standing of working families, the Republican budgets for fiscal year (FY) 2016 would return our economy to the same top-down economics that has failed us before: cutting taxes for millionaires and billionaires, while slashing investments in the middle class that we need to grow the economy, like education, job training, and manufacturing. The Republican proposals stand in stark contrast to the President's FY 2016 Budget, which would bring middle class economics into the 21st Century. A state-by-state breakdown of this contrast, including how the Republican budgets affect Washington, can be found in a report released today here: http://go.wh.gov/RoNU1j.

The President's Budget builds on the progress we've made and shows what we can do if we invest in America's future and commit to an economy that rewards hard work, generates rising incomes, and allows everyone to share in the prosperity of a growing America. It lays out a strategy to strengthen our middle class and help America's hard-working families get ahead in a time of relentless economic and technological change. And it makes the critical investments needed to accelerate and sustain economic growth in the long run, including in research, education, training, and infrastructure.

Republicans have chosen different priorities. Yet again, they are seeking to balance the budget on the backs of the middle class, while cutting taxes for the wealthy and well-connected. They still won't say where many of their spending cuts come from. But they are clear that their budgets would continue the harmful cuts known as sequestration in 2016, threatening economic growth, cutting programs middle-class families count on, and attempting to fund national security through irresponsible budget gimmicks. Their budgets slash domestic investments that support the middle-class even more significantly after 2016, along with programs that serve the most vulnerable Americans. House Republicans would end Medicare as we know it, transforming it from a guarantee seniors can count on into a voucher program. After five years of the Affordable Care Act, more than 16 million people have gained coverage. Yet once again, the Republican budgets propose to repeal the Affordable Care Act's coverage expansions.

The choice could not be more clear or the consequences more stark. Thanks to President Obama and the resilience of the American people, the economy is growing

again. The Republican budgets would put that growth at risk and limit opportunity for the middle-class and those seeking to join it.

In Washington, the Republican budgets would[i]:

Cut Taxes for Millionaires and Raise Taxes for Working Families and Students: While claiming to prioritize fiscal responsibility, the Republican budgets would not ask the wealthy to contribute a single dollar to deficit reduction, and the proposals specified in the House budget would cut taxes for millionaires by an average of at least $50,000. Meanwhile, the Republican budgets do nothing to prevent tax increases averaging $1,100 for 12 million families and students paying for college and $900 for 16 million working families with children. In 2015, 275,000 Washington families will receive a total of $240 million in tax cuts from improvements to pro-work tax credits that would expire after 2017 under the Republican budgets.

Eliminate Affordable Health Care: The Affordable Care Act is working. After five years of the Affordable Care Act, more than 16 million people have gained coverage. Yet once again, the Republican budgets propose to repeal the Affordable Care Act's coverage expansions, taking away health insurance from millions of people. In particular, the Republican budgets would eliminate coverage for 161,000 Washington residents who have newly signed up for coverage or re-enrolled through the Marketplaces. Some of these individuals would become uninsured while others would end up with worse or less affordable coverage.

Raise Health Care Costs for Seniors: 72,400 Washington seniors and people with disabilities benefited by an average of $860 from the closure of the Medicare Part D prescription drug donut hole in 2014 alone. Under the Republican plan to repeal the Affordable Care Act, at least that many would likely have to pay more for needed medications in future years. The House budget would also end Medicare as we know it, replacing guaranteed access to the traditional Medicare program with a voucher program, risking a death spiral in traditional Medicare.

Slash Investments in the Middle Class: Under the Republican budgets, both non-defense and base defense discretionary funding in 2016 would be at the lowest real levels in a decade. Compared to the President's Budget, if the Republican budgets were to take effect, these are just some of the impacts on Washington:

- **Head Start:** 570 fewer children in Washington would have access to Head Start services, representing a permanently missed opportunity to help these children enter elementary school ready to succeed.
- **Teachers and Schools:** Washington would receive $18.7 million less funding for disadvantaged students, an amount that is enough to fund about 70 schools, 260 teacher and aide jobs, and 27,000 students.

- **Education for Children with Disabilities:** Washington would receive $6.4 million less funding to provide educational opportunities for students with disabilities, representing an approximately 2.9 percent cut and shifting the burden for meeting these children's needs to Washington and its local communities.
- **Job Training and Employment Services:** 46,800 fewer Washington residents would receive job training and employment services, including help finding jobs and skills training.
- **Affordable Housing**: Washington would receive approximately $42.7 million less in Federal funding, resulting in 3,200 fewer families receiving Housing Choice Vouchers, which enable very low-income families to afford decent, safe, and sanitary housing in the private market.
- **National Parks:** Construction and renovation projects would be prevented or delayed at five national parks in Washington: Fort Vancouver National Historic Site, Mount Rainier National Park, North Cascades National Park, Olympic National Park, and San Juan Island National Historic Park.

Balances Only with Gimmicks and Deep Cuts to Programs that Serve the Most Vulnerable and Help Expand Opportunity. On top of their cuts to middle-class investments and the ACA, the Republican budgets would cut:

- **Pell Grants:** Republican reductions to Pell would reduce financial aid for the 130,000 Washington students who rely on Pell grants to afford college.
- **Medicaid:** The House Republican proposal to block grant Medicaid would cut Federal funding to Washington by approximately $13.9 billion over ten years, impacting children, seniors, and people with disabilities who rely on Medicaid.
- **Supplemental Nutrition Assistance Program (SNAP):** House Republican proposals to block grant and slash SNAP would cut nutrition aid in Washington by an estimated $2.5 billion over a five year period (2021-2025), jeopardizing nutrition assistance for the 1,096,000 Washington residents who receive SNAP to help them put food on the table.

Fails to Address Our Crumbling Infrastructure: Republican budgets lack a real plan to address the looming expiration and insolvency of the Highway Trust Fund. Through the Highway Trust Fund, in FY 2014 the Federal Government obligated $711.7 million to Washington through the Federal Aid Highways program for highway planning and construction and over $320.2 million through Transit Formula Grants that support our Nation's mass transit systems.

i. Numbers are rounded. For a description of how impacts were calculated, see http://go.wh.gov/RoNU1j

FOR IMMEDIATE RELEASE
March 24, 2015

FACT SHEET: Republican Budget Resolutions: Same Failed Top-Down Economics for West Virginia

With more than 12 million private-sector jobs created over the last 60 months, it is clear that the President's middle class economic agenda is working. But instead of taking the steps we need to strengthen the standing of working families, the Republican budgets for fiscal year (FY) 2016 would return our economy to the same top-down economics that has failed us before: cutting taxes for millionaires and billionaires, while slashing investments in the middle class that we need to grow the economy, like education, job training, and manufacturing. The Republican proposals stand in stark contrast to the President's FY 2016 Budget, which would bring middle class economics into the 21st Century. A state-by-state breakdown of this contrast, including how the Republican budgets affect West Virginia, can be found in a report released today here: http://go.wh.gov/RoNU1j.

The President's Budget builds on the progress we've made and shows what we can do if we invest in America's future and commit to an economy that rewards hard work, generates rising incomes, and allows everyone to share in the prosperity of a growing America. It lays out a strategy to strengthen our middle class and help America's hard-working families get ahead in a time of relentless economic and technological change. And it makes the critical investments needed to accelerate and sustain economic growth in the long run, including in research, education, training, and infrastructure.

Republicans have chosen different priorities. Yet again, they are seeking to balance the budget on the backs of the middle class, while cutting taxes for the wealthy and well-connected. They still won't say where many of their spending cuts come from. But they are clear that their budgets would continue the harmful cuts known as sequestration in 2016, threatening economic growth, cutting programs middle-class families count on, and attempting to fund national security through irresponsible budget gimmicks. Their budgets slash domestic investments that support the middle-class even more significantly after 2016, along with programs that serve the most vulnerable Americans. House Republicans would end Medicare as we know it, transforming it from a guarantee seniors can count on into a voucher program. After five years of the Affordable Care Act, more than 16 million people have gained coverage. Yet once again, the Republican budgets propose to repeal the Affordable Care Act's coverage expansions.

The choice could not be more clear or the consequences more stark. Thanks to President Obama and the resilience of the American people, the economy is growing

again. The Republican budgets would put that growth at risk and limit opportunity for the middle-class and those seeking to join it.

In West Virginia, the Republican budgets would[i]:

Cut Taxes for Millionaires and Raise Taxes for Working Families and Students: While claiming to prioritize fiscal responsibility, the Republican budgets would not ask the wealthy to contribute a single dollar to deficit reduction, and the proposals specified in the House budget would cut taxes for millionaires by an average of at least $50,000. Meanwhile, the Republican budgets do nothing to prevent tax increases averaging $1,100 for 12 million families and students paying for college and $900 for 16 million working families with children. In 2015, 91,000 West Virginia families will receive a total of $76 million in tax cuts from improvements to pro-work tax credits that would expire after 2017 under the Republican budgets.

Eliminate Affordable Health Care: The Affordable Care Act is working. After five years of the Affordable Care Act, more than 16 million people have gained coverage. Yet once again, the Republican budgets propose to repeal the Affordable Care Act's coverage expansions, taking away health insurance from millions of people. In particular, the Republican budgets would eliminate coverage for 33,000 West Virginia residents who have newly signed up for coverage or re-enrolled through the Marketplaces. Some of these individuals would become uninsured while others would end up with worse or less affordable coverage.

Raise Health Care Costs for Seniors: 45,500 West Virginia seniors and people with disabilities benefited by an average of $1,040 from the closure of the Medicare Part D prescription drug donut hole in 2014 alone. Under the Republican plan to repeal the Affordable Care Act, at least that many would likely have to pay more for needed medications in future years. The House budget would also end Medicare as we know it, replacing guaranteed access to the traditional Medicare program with a voucher program, risking a death spiral in traditional Medicare.

Slash Investments in the Middle Class: Under the Republican budgets, both non-defense and base defense discretionary funding in 2016 would be at the lowest real levels in a decade. Compared to the President's Budget, if the Republican budgets were to take effect, these are just some of the impacts on West Virginia:

- **Head Start:** 270 fewer children in West Virginia would have access to Head Start services, representing a permanently missed opportunity to help these children enter elementary school ready to succeed.
- **Teachers and Schools:** West Virginia would receive $7.4 million less funding for disadvantaged students, an amount that is enough to fund about 30 schools, 100 teacher and aide jobs, and 9,000 students.

- **Education for Children with Disabilities:** West Virginia would receive $2.1 million less funding to provide educational opportunities for students with disabilities, representing an approximately 2.8 percent cut and shifting the burden for meeting these children's needs to West Virginia and its local communities.
- **Job Training and Employment Services:** 18,000 fewer West Virginia residents would receive job training and employment services, including help finding jobs and skills training.
- **Affordable Housing**: West Virginia would receive approximately $6.3 million less in Federal funding, resulting in 840 fewer families receiving Housing Choice Vouchers, which enable very low-income families to afford decent, safe, and sanitary housing in the private market.
- **National Parks:** Construction and renovation projects would be prevented or delayed at Harpers Ferry National Historical Park.

Balances Only with Gimmicks and Deep Cuts to Programs that Serve the Most Vulnerable and Help Expand Opportunity. On top of their cuts to middle-class investments and the ACA, the Republican budgets would cut:

- **Pell Grants:** Republican reductions to Pell would reduce financial aid for the 63,000 West Virginia students who rely on Pell grants to afford college.
- **Medicaid:** The House Republican proposal to block grant Medicaid would cut Federal funding to West Virginia by approximately $7.9 billion over ten years, impacting children, seniors, and people with disabilities who rely on Medicaid.
- **Supplemental Nutrition Assistance Program (SNAP):** House Republican proposals to block grant and slash SNAP would cut nutrition aid in West Virginia by an estimated $800 million over a five year period (2021-2025), jeopardizing nutrition assistance for the 363,000 West Virginia residents who receive SNAP to help them put food on the table.

Fails to Address Our Crumbling Infrastructure: Republican budgets lack a real plan to address the looming expiration and insolvency of the Highway Trust Fund. Through the Highway Trust Fund, in FY 2014 the Federal Government obligated $421.0 million to West Virginia through the Federal Aid Highways program for highway planning and construction and over $27.3 million through Transit Formula Grants that support our Nation's mass transit systems.

i. Numbers are rounded. For a description of how impacts were calculated, see http://go.wh.gov/RoNU1j

FOR IMMEDIATE RELEASE
March 24, 2015

FACT SHEET: Republican Budget Resolutions: Same Failed Top-Down Economics for Wisconsin

With more than 12 million private-sector jobs created over the last 60 months, it is clear that the President's middle class economic agenda is working. But instead of taking the steps we need to strengthen the standing of working families, the Republican budgets for fiscal year (FY) 2016 would return our economy to the same top-down economics that has failed us before: cutting taxes for millionaires and billionaires, while slashing investments in the middle class that we need to grow the economy, like education, job training, and manufacturing. The Republican proposals stand in stark contrast to the President's FY 2016 Budget, which would bring middle class economics into the 21st Century. A state-by-state breakdown of this contrast, including how the Republican budgets affect Wisconsin, can be found in a report released today here: http://go.wh.gov/RoNU1j.

The President's Budget builds on the progress we've made and shows what we can do if we invest in America's future and commit to an economy that rewards hard work, generates rising incomes, and allows everyone to share in the prosperity of a growing America. It lays out a strategy to strengthen our middle class and help America's hard-working families get ahead in a time of relentless economic and technological change. And it makes the critical investments needed to accelerate and sustain economic growth in the long run, including in research, education, training, and infrastructure.

Republicans have chosen different priorities. Yet again, they are seeking to balance the budget on the backs of the middle class, while cutting taxes for the wealthy and well-connected. They still won't say where many of their spending cuts come from. But they are clear that their budgets would continue the harmful cuts known as sequestration in 2016, threatening economic growth, cutting programs middle-class families count on, and attempting to fund national security through irresponsible budget gimmicks. Their budgets slash domestic investments that support the middle-class even more significantly after 2016, along with programs that serve the most vulnerable Americans. House Republicans would end Medicare as we know it, transforming it from a guarantee seniors can count on into a voucher program. After five years of the Affordable Care Act, more than 16 million people have gained coverage. Yet once again, the Republican budgets propose to repeal the Affordable Care Act's coverage expansions.

The choice could not be more clear or the consequences more stark. Thanks to President Obama and the resilience of the American people, the economy is growing

again. The Republican budgets would put that growth at risk and limit opportunity for the middle-class and those seeking to join it.

In Wisconsin, the Republican budgets would[i]:

Cut Taxes for Millionaires and Raise Taxes for Working Families and Students: While claiming to prioritize fiscal responsibility, the Republican budgets would not ask the wealthy to contribute a single dollar to deficit reduction, and the proposals specified in the House budget would cut taxes for millionaires by an average of at least $50,000. Meanwhile, the Republican budgets do nothing to prevent tax increases averaging $1,100 for 12 million families and students paying for college and $900 for 16 million working families with children. In 2015, 225,000 Wisconsin families will receive a total of $202 million in tax cuts from improvements to pro-work tax credits that would expire after 2017 under the Republican budgets.

Eliminate Affordable Health Care: The Affordable Care Act is working. After five years of the Affordable Care Act, more than 16 million people have gained coverage. Yet once again, the Republican budgets propose to repeal the Affordable Care Act's coverage expansions, taking away health insurance from millions of people. In particular, the Republican budgets would eliminate coverage for 207,000 Wisconsin residents who have newly signed up for coverage or re-enrolled through the Marketplaces. Some of these individuals would become uninsured while others would end up with worse or less affordable coverage.

Raise Health Care Costs for Seniors: 89,400 Wisconsin seniors and people with disabilities benefited by an average of $910 from the closure of the Medicare Part D prescription drug donut hole in 2014 alone. Under the Republican plan to repeal the Affordable Care Act, at least that many would likely have to pay more for needed medications in future years. The House budget would also end Medicare as we know it, replacing guaranteed access to the traditional Medicare program with a voucher program, risking a death spiral in traditional Medicare.

Slash Investments in the Middle Class: Under the Republican budgets, both non-defense and base defense discretionary funding in 2016 would be at the lowest real levels in a decade. Compared to the President's Budget, if the Republican budgets were to take effect, these are just some of the impacts on Wisconsin:

- **Head Start:** 490 fewer children in Wisconsin would have access to Head Start services, representing a permanently missed opportunity to help these children enter elementary school ready to succeed.
- **Teachers and Schools:** Wisconsin would receive $18.3 million less funding for disadvantaged students, an amount that is enough to fund about 100 schools, 250 teacher and aide jobs, and 25,000 students.

- **Education for Children with Disabilities:** Wisconsin would receive $5.8 million less funding to provide educational opportunities for students with disabilities, representing an approximately 2.8 percent cut and shifting the burden for meeting these children's needs to Wisconsin and its local communities.
- **Job Training and Employment Services:** 40,100 fewer Wisconsin residents would receive job training and employment services, including help finding jobs and skills training.
- **Affordable Housing**: Wisconsin would receive approximately $14.5 million less in Federal funding, resulting in 1,570 fewer families receiving Housing Choice Vouchers, which enable very low-income families to afford decent, safe, and sanitary housing in the private market.
- **National Parks:** Construction and renovation projects would be prevented or delayed at Apostle Islands National Lakeshore.

Balances Only with Gimmicks and Deep Cuts to Programs that Serve the Most Vulnerable and Help Expand Opportunity. On top of their cuts to middle-class investments and the ACA, the Republican budgets would cut:

- **Pell Grants:** Republican reductions to Pell would reduce financial aid for the 117,000 Wisconsin students who rely on Pell grants to afford college.
- **Medicaid:** The House Republican proposal to block grant Medicaid would cut Federal funding to Wisconsin by approximately $14.5 billion over ten years, impacting children, seniors, and people with disabilities who rely on Medicaid.
- **Supplemental Nutrition Assistance Program (SNAP):** House Republican proposals to block grant and slash SNAP would cut nutrition aid in Wisconsin by an estimated $1.8 billion over a five year period (2021-2025), jeopardizing nutrition assistance for the 842,000 Wisconsin residents who receive SNAP to help them put food on the table.

Fails to Address Our Crumbling Infrastructure: Republican budgets lack a real plan to address the looming expiration and insolvency of the Highway Trust Fund. Through the Highway Trust Fund, in FY 2014 the Federal Government obligated $805.5 million to Wisconsin through the Federal Aid Highways program for highway planning and construction and over $178.8 million through Transit Formula Grants that support our Nation's mass transit systems.

###

i. Numbers are rounded. For a description of how impacts were calculated, see http://go.wh.gov/RoNU1j

FOR IMMEDIATE RELEASE
March 24, 2015

FACT SHEET: Republican Budget Resolutions: Same Failed Top-Down Economics for Wyoming

With more than 12 million private-sector jobs created over the last 60 months, it is clear that the President's middle class economic agenda is working. But instead of taking the steps we need to strengthen the standing of working families, the Republican budgets for fiscal year (FY) 2016 would return our economy to the same top-down economics that has failed us before: cutting taxes for millionaires and billionaires, while slashing investments in the middle class that we need to grow the economy, like education, job training, and manufacturing. The Republican proposals stand in stark contrast to the President's FY 2016 Budget, which would bring middle class economics into the 21st Century. A state-by-state breakdown of this contrast, including how the Republican budgets affect Wyoming, can be found in a report released today here: http://go.wh.gov/RoNU1j.

The President's Budget builds on the progress we've made and shows what we can do if we invest in America's future and commit to an economy that rewards hard work, generates rising incomes, and allows everyone to share in the prosperity of a growing America. It lays out a strategy to strengthen our middle class and help America's hard-working families get ahead in a time of relentless economic and technological change. And it makes the critical investments needed to accelerate and sustain economic growth in the long run, including in research, education, training, and infrastructure.

Republicans have chosen different priorities. Yet again, they are seeking to balance the budget on the backs of the middle class, while cutting taxes for the wealthy and well-connected. They still won't say where many of their spending cuts come from. But they are clear that their budgets would continue the harmful cuts known as sequestration in 2016, threatening economic growth, cutting programs middle-class families count on, and attempting to fund national security through irresponsible budget gimmicks. Their budgets slash domestic investments that support the middle-class even more significantly after 2016, along with programs that serve the most vulnerable Americans. House Republicans would end Medicare as we know it, transforming it from a guarantee seniors can count on into a voucher program. After five years of the Affordable Care Act, more than 16 million people have gained coverage. Yet once again, the Republican budgets propose to repeal the Affordable Care Act's coverage expansions.

The choice could not be more clear or the consequences more stark. Thanks to President Obama and the resilience of the American people, the economy is growing

again. The Republican budgets would put that growth at risk and limit opportunity for the middle-class and those seeking to join it.

In Wyoming, the Republican budgets would[i]:

Cut Taxes for Millionaires and Raise Taxes for Working Families and Students: While claiming to prioritize fiscal responsibility, the Republican budgets would not ask the wealthy to contribute a single dollar to deficit reduction, and the proposals specified in the House budget would cut taxes for millionaires by an average of at least $50,000. Meanwhile, the Republican budgets do nothing to prevent tax increases averaging $1,100 for 12 million families and students paying for college and $900 for 16 million working families with children. In 2015, 22,000 Wyoming families will receive a total of $20 million in tax cuts from improvements to pro-work tax credits that would expire after 2017 under the Republican budgets.

Eliminate Affordable Health Care: The Affordable Care Act is working. After five years of the Affordable Care Act, more than 16 million people have gained coverage. Yet once again, the Republican budgets propose to repeal the Affordable Care Act's coverage expansions, taking away health insurance from millions of people. In particular, the Republican budgets would eliminate coverage for 21,000 Wyoming residents who have newly signed up for coverage or re-enrolled through the Marketplaces. Some of these individuals would become uninsured while others would end up with worse or less affordable coverage.

Raise Health Care Costs for Seniors: 7,900 Wyoming seniors and people with disabilities benefited by an average of $850 from the closure of the Medicare Part D prescription drug donut hole in 2014 alone. Under the Republican plan to repeal the Affordable Care Act, at least that many would likely have to pay more for needed medications in future years. The House budget would also end Medicare as we know it, replacing guaranteed access to the traditional Medicare program with a voucher program, risking a death spiral in traditional Medicare.

Slash Investments in the Middle Class: Under the Republican budgets, both non-defense and base defense discretionary funding in 2016 would be at the lowest real levels in a decade. Compared to the President's Budget, if the Republican budgets were to take effect, these are just some of the impacts on Wyoming:

- **Head Start:** 60 fewer children in Wyoming would have access to Head Start services, representing a permanently missed opportunity to help these children enter elementary school ready to succeed.
- **Teachers and Schools:** Wyoming would receive $3.1 million less funding for disadvantaged students, an amount that is enough to fund about 20 schools, 40 teacher and aide jobs, and 2,000 students.

- **Education for Children with Disabilities:** Wyoming would receive $1.3 million less funding to provide educational opportunities for students with disabilities, representing an approximately 4.5 percent cut and shifting the burden for meeting these children's needs to Wyoming and its local communities.
- **Job Training and Employment Services:** 12,200 fewer Wyoming residents would receive job training and employment services, including help finding jobs and skills training.
- **Affordable Housing**: Wyoming would receive approximately $1.3 million less in Federal funding, resulting in 140 fewer families receiving Housing Choice Vouchers, which enable very low-income families to afford decent, safe, and sanitary housing in the private market.
- **National Parks:** Construction and renovation projects would be prevented or delayed at five national parks in Wyoming: Bighorn Canyon National Recreation Area, Fort Laramie National Historic Site, Yellowstone National Park, Bighorn Canyon National Recreation Area, and Grand Teton National Park.

Balances Only with Gimmicks and Deep Cuts to Programs that Serve the Most Vulnerable and Help Expand Opportunity. On top of their cuts to middle-class investments and the ACA, the Republican budgets would cut:

- **Pell Grants:** Republican reductions to Pell would reduce financial aid for the 12,000 Wyoming students who rely on Pell grants to afford college.
- **Medicaid:** The House Republican proposal to block grant Medicaid would cut Federal funding to Wyoming by approximately $1.0 billion over ten years, impacting children, seniors, and people with disabilities who rely on Medicaid.
- **Supplemental Nutrition Assistance Program (SNAP):** House Republican proposals to block grant and slash SNAP would cut nutrition aid in Wyoming by an estimated $100 million over a five year period (2021-2025), jeopardizing nutrition assistance for the 36,000 Wyoming residents who receive SNAP to help them put food on the table.

Fails to Address Our Crumbling Infrastructure: Republican budgets lack a real plan to address the looming expiration and insolvency of the Highway Trust Fund. Through the Highway Trust Fund, in FY 2014 the Federal Government obligated $257.0 million to Wyoming through the Federal Aid Highways program for highway planning and construction and over $21.1 million through Transit Formula Grants that support our Nation's mass transit systems.

###

i. Numbers are rounded. For a description of how impacts were calculated, see http://go.wh.gov/RoNU1

www.ingramcontent.com/pod-product-compliance
Lightning Source LLC
Chambersburg PA
CBHW080252290526
45790CB00005B/1782